THE HONEY BADGER GUIDE TO LIFE

HONEY BADGER

For more about Nick Cummins,
download 'The Honey Badger' app
available on:

Follow Nick's adventures at @nckcmmns on Twitter,
@nickbadger on Instagram
or facebook.com/NickCumminsSays

THE HONEY BADGER GUIDE TO LIFE

NICK CUMMINS

With help from my old man Mark

MACMILLAN
Pan Macmillan Australia

First published 2018 in Macmillan by Pan Macmillan Australia Pty Ltd
1 Market Street, Sydney, New South Wales, Australia, 2000

Cataloguing-in-Publication entry is available
from the National Library of Australia
http://catalogue.nla.gov.au

Typeset in 12/18.5 pt Bembo by Midland Typesetters, Australia
Printed by McPherson's Printing Group
Chapter illustrations courtesy of shutterstock. Photographs on
pages vi, x, 15, 52, 93, 97, 110, 131, 148, 164, 178 and 192 used with
kind permission from Dan Boud Photography. Photographs on pages 6
and 12–16 of picture section courtesy of Nick Cummins. Photographs on
pages 1–5 and 7–11 of picture section and pages xiii and 101 used with
kind permission from National Geographic Australia - Dan Walkington.
Shortcummins, 'The Chub Hotel', 'The Cats in the Cradle',
'Rum Mathematics' and 'Bearded Macadamias' used with kind
permission from Cummins Diverse Investments Pty Ltd.

This book is dedicated to Australians who stand up, face life head-on, take the hits, then get back up and go again. Well done, cobbers.

CONTENTS

Foreword by Mark Cummins, father of The Badger

How much do you enjoy a cool breeze on a warm summer's day? This is Nick Cummins – a refreshing change to our straight up and down existence.

Nick says the things we would like to say and does the things we would only dream of doing.

Barriers and standard conventions don't affect his attitude or resilience. Rules aren't being broken but they are certainly being bent.

On the rugby field, Nick had the ability to set the crowd alight with hard running and a fearless, uncompromising boldness. Crowds around the world applauded his skill and determination.

Off the field his 'why not' approach and love of Aussie culture has seen him eagerly embrace adventure in all its forms. Thankfully, in books like this he takes us along for the ride.

From reindeer racing in Norway to shark-diving in South Australia and a hundred adventures in-between – if it's there to be done, he'll do it.

Armed with a ute-load of humour and a personality to match, Nick reminds us of the slowly disappearing fair dinkum Aussie.

His concerns that Australian men are losing themselves in our tightly controlled PC culture only pushes him more and more to encourage others to be themselves, not who others want them to be.

He encourages blokes to find themselves, reach their full potential and to be happy in their own skin.

Nick's a funny bugger – he sees the good in people and the humour in everything.

Loyalty and love of family and friends are the banner under which he serves.

Many years from now he'll be sitting on his veranda nursing his grandkids, telling stories of a life well led. His experiences will open their eyes to the wonder of Australia and the uniqueness of our history.

But that's in the future, he's only just started.

Nick 'The Honey Badger' Cummins has evolved into a balance of talent and humility. Australia needs him.

His proud old man
Mark

THE MEANING
OF LIFE

We're born kicking and screaming and then latch on for a feed. If we're lucky, we're loved, and depend on our parents for everything. As we kick on, we learn good and bad from family and friends and try to find our spot on the planet. As a young bloke discovers girls, he realises that his weapon is not just good for dangling soap on a rope or hanging a towel (gifted blokes only). Eventually, most fellas tie the knot or shack up with their princess, have kids and put on weight. After a standard life, we pull the pin and face the Big Fella. Then when we're done, the kids can blue over what's left.

That's a pretty average summary of life, but it doesn't have to be like that. Our lives can be so much better. Life is a gift and we should grab it with both hands and enjoy the shit out of it. Bear with me, and we'll go into a bit more detail.

Hatch: The Wonder Years

Having a youngster is a pretty big deal. For previous generations, having a truckload of kids was the norm. Huge families were the order of the day, it's just the way it was. I'm from a big family and I enjoyed my time as a youngster. As one of eight kids, you learnt to be a little less selfish, that you can't always have what you want and to be a little more patient. Mostly, you learnt to be on time for tucker.

Life was pretty simple. As a youngster, whatever my oldies said was the truth, but I still had some doubts about Santa, and I was positive the Easter Bunny was a rort. Still, I liked chocolate, so I ran with it.

As I climbed the age ladder, I found some gaps in my parents' knowledge and luckily I was able to fill those gaps by asking why and why not. I became sharper and more creative, and this led to some cunning moves.

When I was about fourteen, I was having a blue with my younger sister Alicia and managed to shatter her dreams when I told her I'd just killed the Easter Bunny with my bow and arrow. Sure, it was a low act, but it was payback. She'd dobbed me in for shooting her inflatable dolphin with the same weapon. I apologised for my act of vengeance last year.

Growing up can be tough at times, but it's through the tough times that we learn some great lessons. We need to bottom-out before we start to really grow up. We need to navigate through the hard times gaining and using knowledge to prepare us for what life throws at us. When we're young, we want to be like everyone else, we want to fit in. As we get older, we realise we need to be ourselves. No bullshit, this is me and this is how it is.

Some cats make a real effort to stand out. One rooster I know has a haircut like the second-last of the Mohicans, while another looks like he fell face-first into a tackle box. Some just ink up with tough stickers. Your call, but you don't have to look different to be different. We are free to think and feel how we wish. When Nelson Mandela was asked how he didn't go mad after so many years in captivity, he simply said that while they had imprisoned his body, he was the captain of his soul.

Match: Love & Marriage

You know the deal: blokes are amateur birdwatchers, always on the hunt for the red-headed and double-breasted warbler.

Some people have some pretty entertaining stories, always a lot funnier if they didn't happen to you. Love rears its ugly head and we're buggered. I've seen the toughest of blokes go to bits over this love thing; it's a powerful drug. Most people eventually commit to that super someone. Some blokes are just waiting to hear that special sentence, 'I'd rather be your wife than have a meaningful existence.' Doesn't that just warm the heart?

Seriously though, a good mate of mine gets hitched this year. After years together, Blair and Jen decided to make it legal. Blair is definitely punching above, but has confirmed that his wife-to-be has 20–20 vision and a good sense of smell. It must be love! I've known them both for years and they've got the chemistry right. No ownership, no one takes the lead, just two people who move in the same direction – full steam ahead.

Dispatch: Death & Legacy

We're all eventually going to cark it, kiss the concrete, pull the pin, go wheels up, lights out or whatever you want to call it. It seems a bit arse-up that after we acquire a lifetime of knowledge and experience, we snuff it.

So it's bloody important to live, not just exist!

Don't sell yourself short, have a crack at many things, surround yourself with positive people. Travel, laugh, cry, get the shits and learn to get over yourself quickly. Take a calculated risk. Love yourself and don't judge or expect too much from others. Don't be one of those people who leave it till the end to apologise for all life's indiscretions, when a few words at the right time could have meant years of joy and understanding. Make your peace along the way. Tell people you're sorry and tell the special people in your life that you love them. Do you want to be right or be happy? You choose.

Don't lose sleep over loot! There's no pockets in coffins, so why be the richest bastard in the graveyard? Enjoy your hard-earned brass.

You get one shot at this fantastic world, don't cock it up.

Each day is a gift, so tomorrow morning when you drag your busted arse out of the cot, make a decision to have a good day. Forget the little things because in the end they don't matter. What matters is how much you've loved. But clean your teeth for God's sake, so people don't dry retch when you smile at them.

The Honey Badger Guide to Life # 1

Love yourself – we're all good units. If we love ourselves, we will love others.

REFLECTIONS

I'm not really religious. I was raised a Catholic but the roof would probably fall in if I went marching down the church aisle now.

That said, I reckon I'm a spiritual person. I believe there is something more to life than waking up in the morning, going to work for 60-odd years, watching TV for another ten, then going wheels-up.

We're put on this planet for a reason, and we've got to find it.

We all need loot and love, but we need to give a bit to get a bit. The more you do for others, the more good things come your way, usually.

I've had a wild ride so far, full of great times and disappointments. Through all that, I'm still finding my way.

When I was playing rugby, I worked bloody hard, and finally played for the Wallabies. Broken bones, occasional poor form and self-doubt all combined to make me ask the big question: do I keep at this or is it too hard?

When I first started playing Super Rugby with the Western Force, I really battled with the workload. It got to a stage where I didn't think I could take the pre-season punishment. Thirty-five-degree heat, sand hills, contact sessions with gorillas disguised as forwards, vomiting, wrestling, crawling into bed at night absolutely shagged . . . then doing it all again the next day.

Getting injured was almost seen as weakness. One game in 2009, I broke my leg and dislocated my ankle at the same time. I was in a helluva lot of pain, and I remember the trainer saying to me, 'Come on, Nick, ten more minutes, you can do it.' I looked at him through the agony and begged God to give me the strength to strangle the bastard.

One night, I rang the old man to talk about how hard it was. He gave me the option of coming home and working as a labourer for his landscaping company. Whether he meant it or not, that gave me the jolt I needed. The rest is history. Sometimes, we all need a dose of reality. And sure enough, the harder I worked, the more the rewards came.

We all have stages in our lives where we hit obstacles, and it seems too hard to go on. It can be work, health, relationships – all manner of things. I've learnt to not over-think it.

Take your time, have a spell and a cry if you need it. Gather your thoughts and strength, and go again. As the old fella says, the sun always comes up tomorrow.

Well-meaning people will always tell you, 'you'll be right,' but they have no idea what you're going through or how you feel about the situation. Only people who have experienced the same struggles as you will understand. They don't judge; they want to help.

Remember that no one has your vision. The way you see things is unique, and while some will understand, the vast majority will just pay lip service.

But, as my uncle once said: many are cold, few are frozen. Don't think poorly of those people because we can all be a bit ignorant.

Whatever you do in life, you will have doubters. Whether it's in your own week-to-week world or on life's big stage, some people have a need to bring you down. Unfortunately, in Australia, we sometimes seem to want to drag back the frontrunners, like we're in a 5000 metre race. Slowly but surely, we pull them back to the pack.

Americans cheer the winner while Aussies tend to cheer the underdog. While this is usually a good thing, sometimes people can become jealous of success. The keyboard warriors are a good example, sitting behind a laptop, tearing people to bits. They don't know the people they're slandering;

they just get their jollies out of causing grief. I almost feel sympathy for the bastards.

If this is you, well, it's not too late to change tack. It's so easy to be caught up in these witch hunts and character assassinations – usually media-driven. We're better than that.

We all need to make a personal stand against this behaviour because the universe is watching, and what goes around comes around. The Aussie way is to give people a fair go.

It's like throwing a rock in a pond. A small action, a change of heart, will ripple out to others. Who knows how far it will go? No one is perfect and we all fail, but if we try just that little bit we can make our families, friends, communities and the whole bloody country a better place.

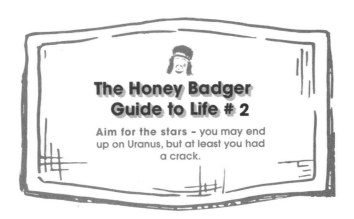

The Honey Badger Guide to Life # 2

Aim for the stars – you may end up on Uranus, but at least you had a crack.

Life is about struggle and, through those tough times, we will find our purpose. Do you know why old buggers sit there and smile? Because they've worked it out.

Back in my old Catholic Church altar-boy days (I didn't mind the red wine), we had a sacrament called Confession. I wasn't keen on it because you had to tell the priest about all your current sins. But it didn't matter what you'd done, you just ripped out twenty *Hail Marys* and all was forgiven.

One priest, after listening to a list of my many crimes against humanity, replied, 'Mate, just be the best you can be.'

Now, that's a bloke who gets it.

Like a bag of cats at a greyhound meet

(luyk-uh-bag-ov-kats-at-uh-grayhownd-meet)

Uncertainty, distress, high anxiety, pressure, feeling the pinch

Common usage: *They ran out of booze and we were sweatin' like a bag of cats at a greyhound meet.*

A DIFFERENT KIND OF SERVE

Growing up meant pushing the boundaries. In a big family, that meant opportunities to get into strife and then push the blame towards someone else.

Getting a smack on the arse was both painful and embarrassing, so any act that may bring retribution needed an escape route. The truth was always the first victim in my quest to avoid punishment.

My older brothers had an extra couple of years of cunning misdeeds on me, and were too experienced to be framed, and my sisters were armed to the teeth with female awareness. My younger brothers, however, were just novices in this area. That made them the perfect fall guys. I'd even go as far as to bribe Jake and Joe, but they had a tendency to break under questioning, so this master criminal was usually found out.

One Monday coming home from school, I was filthy because I'd been kept in at lunchtime. The bastards, I would have done my homework eventually!

Dad arrived home and he was filthy as well. I was sure he would have done his homework too!

After a terse exchange, I decided I was not in the mood for a serve and I decided I was old enough not to take anything from this bugger.

Hell, I was fourteen and knew a fair bit!

After throwing some pretty average chat his way, he just looked at me and pointed to the shed. My heart sank quicker than the *Titanic*.

Now, the shed by itself wasn't a bad place. It contained Dad's office, boat and all his work gear. Being about 15 m × 12 m, it was a great place to muck about. I'd never seen it as a place of execution until now.

Slowly, I trailed him up to the torture chamber, having visions of fires burning and steam hissing. My God, what had I done? As we walked in, Dad said, 'Shut the door,' and the words had the same effect as signing off on my last will and testament.

I was only a kid, with much to live for. I wasn't ready to die, especially in a shed with a crazed father of eight!

What galah said what doesn't kill you makes you stronger? I wish I could swap with that bastard. Was it too late to apologise?

The old man looked at me with tired eyes and said, 'Mate, I want you to tell me what you're filthy about and why you think I'm such a prick. Have your say, I'll listen. Get it off your chest.'

Well, hello! The shoe was on the other foot. I'm away! After picking up momentum, I gave it to him with both barrels. All the real and imagined evils he had perpetrated on this wisdom packed fourteen-year-old came to the surface. How good did I feel!

After this dictator-like tirade he told me to get two beers out of the fridge. After his first sip, he said to me calmly, 'I'm your father and there is much I could say to you but I'm wiser and I love you. You will never speak to me this way again. Let's drink this beer and remember this day.'

In some ways, I would've preferred imminent death. Even now, I still think about his words. He really got to me that day.

BADGERSAURUS

Don't throw a tantrum . . .

Chuck a wobbly

Have a spak attack

Do your block

Go off ya scone

Blow your stack

Go troppo

Blow a fuse

Flip your lid

Spit the dummy

BADGERSAURUS

ROGUE CHAMPIONS

Some roosters stand out in life. Whether it be good luck, good management or great courage, they become champions to us all.

Some sportspeople get our attention because of feats of endurance and skill. We ride the highs and lows with these inspirational people, as they give us something to admire.

Sometimes we hear the backstory of doers and dreamers that have made our country great, but not often enough. We need more of this. So, strap yourselves in punters, because in this book I'm going to highlight some bloody champions who, despite all their trouble and strife, waded through the naysayers (displaying elephant-sized nuts) to become Rogue Champions.

© Australian War Memorial

Private Bruce Steel Kingsbury VC

Bruce started off as we all do – he was born. He made his way through school without too much grief and went to TAFE College. He got bored with that pretty quickly and left to become a real estate agent. He got even more bored with that and left to work on a property in Western Victoria. You guessed it: he got bored with that too, so he and his mate, Alan, decided to walk the 900 kms to Sydney. They picked up jobs along the way to keep them in tucker and probably a few beers, and arrived in Sydney, totally shagged.

What was his next plan? Well, Bruce and Alan jumped on the next train home. This adventure thing was way over-rated! Bruce finally settled down to help the old man sell real estate.

Then along came World War II. In 1940, Bruce decided to have a crack, and enlisted in the Second Australian Imperial Force. In 1941, he was in the Middle East, fighting the Vichy French, a crowd who had sided with the Nazis. Bruce and his mates had cleaned them up and were called home just in time. The Japanese had declared war and were heading south to pick up some prime Aussie real estate.

In August 1942, Bruce and the young fellas of the 2/14th Infantry Battalion were sent to New Guinea to relieve the Australian militia men who had been holding fort. Darwin had been bombed earlier that year, and most of its townspeople had broken the world land-speed record to Adelaide. Australia was in deep shit.

On the Kokoda Track, Australian forces were outnumbered six to one.

Australia needed something special. Cometh the hour, cometh the man.

On 29 August, Bruce's company was overrun by hundreds of Japan's finest. They were a brave and fearless enemy, more than willing to die for the emperor. Bruce was more than willing to help them achieve that goal.

As the right flank caved, Bruce drew breath, grabbed a Bren gun from a wounded mate and attacked.

He didn't look much, clothing and boots rotted off, and suffering from malaria.

Bruce charged into the horde of attackers, killing dozens and completely wrecking the advance. If that wasn't enough, he chased what was left of Japan's finest into the jungle. A captured Japanese officer's diary described Bruce as a 'God-like warrior who struck fear into our hearts'. The Aussie troops rallied and followed this great man until the day was won. As the troops returned to their positions, a single shot rang out. Bruce was dead before he hit the ground, shot by a sniper. His great mate, Alan Avery, carried his body back. Bruce was later buried in Bomana Cemetery in New Guinea. His mates were inconsolable.

Bruce Steel Kingsbury was awarded the Victoria Cross for courage above and beyond. He was one tough bastard, who stood up when it counted.

We could learn a lot from Bruce.

TAKING A HORN FROM THE BULL

Scars can be a good reminder of adventure. Some highlight shenanigans gone silly – teenage skylarking that took to the skies, or a loose and late night bending the elbow with good mates. These lines of reattached skin tend to come with a decent yarn.

I've managed a few dings in the chassis over time, though the best of the body's barnacles would be a long and wide number which arcs across the side of my ribcage. I scored it on a trip to the NT recently.

I was on this remote property below River Station,

helping out with the herding of some buffalo and seeing how some blokes go about their days.

So, I'm out there in this remote scrubby area, belting about in these armoured four-wheel drives with no roofs and these full metal arms hanging off the side, and a chopper flying low overhead. It was like *Jurassic Park*, and it was hectic.

It's nonstop, all day, every day. And these blokes just get on with it, starting early and working to 9 pm some nights, with a twenty-minute kip under a tree for lunch. These fellas were harder than some of the bulls we were herding, and I will never forget their approach to things – get in and get on with it.

To herd these wild beasts, you have to run them into an area and then tie 'em to a tree, from which they get loaded up from the cars onto trucks.

After a few days, I'm feeling the blood run through all areas of The Badger – I'm outdoors, I'm working hard, I'm experiencing the earth and I'm learning something new.

This one day we got a whole heap of these bulls tied off and waiting to be loaded up, and I'm keeping an eye on them, I'm aware their blood is also pumping and they're eyeing off this strange-looking fella just as I've got me lasers on them. And I'm pretty damn aware that these big beasts can pull the ropes, create a bit of slack on the line and have a crack.

At one point, there were two tied to trees that were probably 15 metres away from me. I was walking between them, watching this one bull 'cause he was looking straight at me. The other bull on the other side was behind a tree, staring as well, but I just thought, 'He's behind the tree, he's not interested.' But they're a lot smarter than that.

Then, as I'm watching the first fella, I hear this da-da da-da da-da da-da. I look to my left and see this bull belting at me – he's two metres away and should have been booked for speeding.

I think things through pretty bloody quickly, let me tell ya. I'm thinking about hitting the deck, as at least then I'll miss the horns but then if he's off the rope – and I'd seen 'em get off, it does happen – and I'm on the ground, he'll gore me and stomp me and just ragdoll me until I'm wheezing me last.

The other option is to run and take the horn from the bull. In a split-second, I quickly cover the vitals. Then ... BANG. There was a popping sound as it went in through me back. The horn just missed my kidney. Then the bull was pulling on the tree, at the end of his rope, staring me down. He's pissed – I could see it in his eyes. And now I'm pissed too, working on adrenalin and wanting to shoot the bastard. Then I realise that he's just being a bull, I was annoying him, and full respect to it.

I put my hand to my back and manage to sink two digits straight into a hole that wasn't there that morning. 'Yeah, you got me you bastard,' I say to the bull still staring at me. 'Well done.'

I go back over to the car and the blokes are like, 'You alright?'

'Yeah, yeah, I'm all good.' I didn't think it was that bad – I was hoping it wasn't anyway and I didn't want to tell 'em, because we're working out in the middle of bloody nowhere and I didn't want to hold 'em up. Then I'm also thinking that if I'm not alright and I pass out, then that's going to screw things up even worse.

One of the boys comes over and has a look. He lifts up my shirt and goes, 'Oh, shit.' That wasn't what I wanted to hear – much like being force-fed ABBA on a hangover. 'We gotta get you out of here now, Badge.'

Then he tells old mate in the truck, and he's going, 'Get the bloody chopper in now – we need an extraction. We need The Badger to get out now, now, now!'

So I jump in the chopper, the claret still coming out at a steady click, and we go back to the homestead. As luck would have it, there's a Cessna-210 there as it had just dropped off some supplies. I jump a lift back to Kununurra, where I land at what they say is an airport, but there's not much there and definitely no taxis about. So I end up trekking a few Ks to the local emergency department. There, I take a seat, tell 'em I've got a small cut that may need some stitching and wait for my name to be called.

This is a story that literally scarred me but you need your own stories to tell, and you sure as hell ain't collecting them at a café, staring into a phone and swiping a finger.

THE IMPORTANCE OF A YARN

You know that bloke who walks into the pub with swagger? That guy right there has stories because he's lived. And that bloke knows how to tell his stories.

I reckon we're all missing out on life, wasting time on insignificant shit that doesn't lead to life experience or learning, or provide each of us with a swag of decent yarns.

Stories are important – they speak of who we are and what we're about and where we've come from. Indigenous cultures all over the world know that, and they place incredible importance on their stories.

It's time we took the bull by the horns – or headbutt the shark, another story I can easily fish from my arsenal of experience – and work on our storytelling. The first thing to twig to is there's storytelling and there's *storytelling*. A bloke can come up to me and start yarning over a few shandies. Then I can head bush and another bloke can then give me that same story and drop me in hysterics with the way he goes about it. Good storytelling is about delivery, timing, punchlines and pauses. All these things build, and all these little skills are worth mastering. You've got to be able to stand up and talk with confidence, reach for a glass and give it the old *ding, ding, ding*.

But even with expert delivery, good storytelling starts with life experience. Without it, you've got an empty backpack.

I get that standing up and speaking publicly has many blokes packing it. They're petrified at even the thought of it. And here's the thing – I was never a fan of it myself. I never enjoyed getting up and talking in front of people or to the media. To be honest, I didn't like people much and had some trust issues. I always felt they were taking something from me in getting me to talk and to tell my tales.

But you've got to fight whatever the fear may be. You've got to – because fear is a heavy cloak to wear, it stops you from achieving.

The best way to learn, I reckon, is to throw yourself smack into the middle of a situation. This means getting up and delivering a story or a speech . . . and stuffing it up. Because you *will* stuff it up. And that's ok, because without failure there is absolutely no growth. If you have the fear of stuffing it up, then you're not going to get up and do it, and you're not going to learn and grow.

Get your story sorted. Get up and stuff it up. Practise it in front of the mirror and then get up and stuff it up again. You'll learn each time how you can do it better – and after ten times, or ten years, whatever it is, you'll begin to get it right. You'll have a shot of confidence because you've come to own your stories and you know you've ballsed up before and it didn't actually matter.

You'll eventually become a master yarn-spinner. You'll be the bloke with a bloody good set of stories, the one who can give a solid speech, the fella who's lived and who can share his experiences with others. And that's proper living. And learning.

SHORTCUMMINS

Ripsnorter

(ripsnawtuh)

Havin' a blinder, goin' great guns, dominating, great mark, good hit, jackknifing header

Common usage: *That goal by Ablett was a ripsnorter!*

SHORTCUMMINS

THE BEST MEDICINE

In the course of writing this book I was hit with some bad news.

A mate of mine was officially struck off as a medical professional due to an indiscretion. After seven years of intense training and hard work his career was done and dusted.

His crime? He'd slept with one of his patients.

The fact they were good friends didn't matter to his employers.

The reality now is that my mate can no longer work in the profession he loves. The bloke is shattered. What a waste of time, effort, training and money.

Such a shame — he's a nice fella and was a brilliant vet.

WEDDING ETIQUETTE & BEING THE MAN (THE BEST ONE)

Many bad decisions have been made at weddings. These ceremonies of love and commitment are minefields of social etiquette – especially late in the reception. Here's The Honey Badger's survival guide ...

How many times has a great wedding celebration been torpedoed by a random Christmas grip or a full-freight French kiss on a well-oiled bridesmaid? Oh, yes, it's a dangerous environment alright.

I've witnessed weddings where blokes are only there to pick up, hoping to cash in on a recently single bird who has been poorly treated by some low bastard.

Sometimes, you can smell relationship grief a mile off. Two sets of relatives and friends facing each other across the room, like the Germans and Russians in World War II.

This has got to stop!

My brother Nathan was married in Norway last year. He married a great bird, Elinor, and it was a beautiful day. Things got a bit dodgy when Karl the best man stated that Nathan moved on to Elinor quicker than the Nazis came through Norway. (Not a crack-up if you're Norwegian.) Fortunately, the Norwegians are a forgiving lot when they get pissed and the night was a winner.

In an effort to stop some weddings going south, I feel it's my duty to assist blokes and birds to navigate these dangerous waters. Here's the Cummins drum . . .

What to wear

➤ It's written on the invite, you dumb bastard, so just read it. Usually a bag of fruit (suit), tie optional. If you're waving money about like a bloke with no arms, Vinnies is open until 4 pm on Saturdays for emergency purchases.

➔ Leave your best pair of pluggers at home unless the wedding is in Bali. Don't dress to stand out, or every weird thing you do during the night will be noticed.

The ceremony

➔ The bride must be late, God bless 'em. This is to show the groom what to expect for the rest of his life.

➔ Load up on Beroccas or smoothies in the morning. You'll either avoid a hangover or shit yourself – a 50–50 proposition.

➔ Tell the bride she's beautiful, even if you think her parachute mustn't have opened. It's not about you.

➔ Tell the groom he's the luckiest man on earth. Phrase it in a way that he'll believe you when you say it. Mates usually know when one is lying, so be careful.

The Honey Badger Guide to Life # 3

Punctuality – it's a sign of respect.
Always be on time.

Reception

➤ Do not get blind and vomit. No good can come from chunder under the main table.

➤ No heckling old people or minorities – poor form.

➤ Personally congratulate the bride and groom.

➤ Leave your kit on, especially if the night is cold or the aircon is turned down.

➤ Always use cutlery, and start from the outside. Don't fall for a butter knife duel.

➤ Talk to all the old birds. They usually have a lot of wisdom, like which young sheilas are available.

➤ Don't have a lash at any of the bride's immediate family. Cousins are fair game.

Be the best man

As best man, you're wearing the captain's arm band and you're calling the shots. You can make this a great day or you can cock it up big time. Your mission starts the night before.

➤ Make the groom hit the sack early.

➤ Reassure him that with antibiotics, the stinging sensation will pass.

➤ Stroke his forehead (only) until he lapses into a coma.

➤ Next morning, ignore the first alarm, think about the second and react violently to the third.

➤ Get him a coffee and don't start the big day with, 'Well, it was nice while it lasted.'

➤ Help dress the poor bastard. Remember shirt before pants, pants before shoes, tie before jacket.

The rings

Forget these, and you may as well do what you're told during a Qantas safety talk – lean forward as far as you can, brace for impact and kiss your arse goodbye.

The speech

For a best man, this is the deal breaker. The crowd is typically pretty well-lubricated at this stage of the night, so will usually ignore some questionable innuendo and forgive some feralisms.

But the speech must be free-flowing with no mention of the groom's former conquests or his time in Turkish prison. For God's sake, focus on his achievements instead.

No bride jokes. You know the one about why women have small feet – so they can stand closer to the sink. Or why the bride wears white – so she can match the kitchen appliances. Or that old chestnut about marriage being about give and take – get ready to give because she's gonna take. These are no-go zones. Go easy on the turps, and make sure you compliment everyone. Toast the bride, groom, the bridesmaids, all the assembled family and friends and heads of state and smile. What could possibly go wrong?

Giggle suit
(giguhl-sooht)

Clothing, bag-of-fruit suit, attire, clobber, kit, get-up, lycra suit, luring kit, freak show

Common usage: *A quick sh*t, shower and shave, then slap on the giggle suit and I'm there.*

GET YOUR BUNIONS
IN THE BUSH

Get. Off. The. Grid.

These are four very simple words, but not enough of us are tackling them and getting out amongst it.

I was lucky to have a childhood surrounded by space. It meant belting about the bush and being engaged with what sits all around us, not navigating the rat race of concrete and glass. It meant coming to understand the power of nature and how the great outdoors can set you right.

We're too often lost in our screens, staring at shit that I guarantee doesn't make one difference to your life.

It's why I go bush whenever I can. I take off the

toe-coverings and plant my canal boats in the dirt. More than that – I head to the outback and find a patch of earth and lie down.

Call me a hippy if you want – I don't care. I know the power of the earth – and it's my power just as much as it's your power. The nature that packs this great earth of ours is a great source of happiness, energy and wellbeing.

Studies on this by people wearing actual white lab coats have been done for years. And people wandering about the earth felt it long before.

Personally, I've realised I can alter my own energy by getting outdoors, and it's all to do with these things called ions. They're all around you these ions, in the air and water and on the ground.

Now, to confuse matters, it's the positive ions that you don't want – they're the ones that can lead to negative emotions, anxiety and feeling flatter than a brown snake catching some rays on the Pacific Highway. What you need to feel tip-top are negative ions. And it's been proven that they tend to hang out in large numbers in the bush, packed into forests, on beaches and near waterfalls. In fact, they reckon the bases of waterfalls are overflowing with these happy little bastards.

I learnt a bit about all this on a lost trip to Mongolia. In fact, I ended up rolling about in the dirt a few times over there, when we were chasing this eagle hunter bloke around. These guys all spoke of the power of the earth and how to get amongst it, about how the animals all do it, and so it was necessary The Badger got into it too.

Now, you don't have to go chasing blokes in some strange get-up across far-flung fields in outer Asia to feel this. Think about the release you get when you grab a stick and belt down to the beach to get wet after a shit day in the office questioning what you've actually done with your life, and how it is you've ended up wearing a giggle suit and speaking in acronyms and business chat (and you all think I speak funny)!

But hit the water and you immediately get a sense of relief. That's because the waves are packed, churning around and smashing about with negative ions, and they wash off all the positive (bad) ions you bring into the sea. This is why it's hard to have a stressed time surfing – even if some little grommet with straw for hair keeps dropping in or going the snake. It doesn't matter – it's calming because your ions are balancing out. Even if you just sit out the back and don't catch a wave, you're feeling better than you did a couple of clicks earlier.

It's the same in the bush. Go for a walk in a forest and breathe in the negative ions. If you can, find a waterfall and give your getaway sticks a break and just take it in. If you can get to the top of a mountain, do that too.

I have to live in Sydney these days because it's where I'm meant to be at this time – and the big smoke can get to me. But when I can I get away, get off the grid and go bush.

It's where I recharge and get away from the distractions. I know when I get out there and get amongst nature, I breathe better, think clearer and I get back to being me.

The other great thing about getting off the grid and going bush is learning more about yourself. Because you've got yourself in a situation that's new and you're not used to, learning comes belting through the front door.

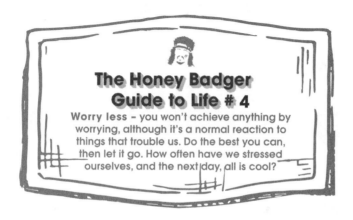

The Honey Badger Guide to Life # 4

Worry less – you won't achieve anything by worrying, although it's a normal reaction to things that trouble us. Do the best you can, then let it go. How often have we stressed ourselves, and the next day, all is cool?

MY ROGUE GENTLEMEN'S CLUB

I'm the leader of a Rogue Gentlemen's Club. I take a bunch of blokes away to these nature spots – we've got these islands and a farm – and they have to get their shoes off and stick their phones away in a box.

With all that connection to social media and online bullshit completely gone, it actually takes them a day or so to detox from their devices, even longer for some. But we go out there, and go on these little missions throughout the day. We need to start camp, and then we need to get the fire going and we also need to get some tucker for the night. Simple stuff, but practical. And powerful.

Of course we need tucker too. And on an island or some reef, there's fish everywhere. But some of these blokes have only ever caught their dinner down the local Coles or Maccas. So, I sit with them and show them. Baiting up, casting out, testing the line, feeling for the fish. And then he's got it – he's learning. And then when he's got a little fish, we use that to get a bigger fish, and he's now part of this process and it's also helping him cut all the cyber thoughts that he has every day. I'm removing this bloke from the fake world and getting him into the real world – 'cause what's more real than a man needing to learn how to hunt and gather so he can actually eat that night?

It's basic, it's primal and it's real. And then he's sitting on the beach, showing how to gut and clean and fillet. He's on his knees in the sand, feeling all the power that comes from the earth, and concentrating on something that is the most important thing going on.

At that point, that bloke is grounded in his power. He doesn't realise it yet, but his power is building. And then we're setting up the fire and showing him how to cook the fish, and why he wants to do it with hot rocks and this is how he gets them hot and these are the methods we're using to cook it and these are the herbs we're bunging on the fish. And then we're sitting around the fire and reminiscing about the day, talking about stuff and everyone's connecting.

We connect with the earth and we connect with each other. We swap stories and we laugh and we have, finally, switched off. We've powered up on our positivity and we're connected with stuff that is real.

And this is why you need to get off the grid and go rogue.

If you want me to give you the sales pitch for my Rogue Gentlemen's Club, then it's this:

Have you lost direction in life?

Have you lost the eye of the tiger?

Do you want to gain or regain your passion for life?

Time to get on board, because that's what the Rogue Gentlemen's Club is about – helping you stoke that fire in the belly with some time in the bush to get off the grid, and get plugged in to the things that really count.

I hope that people who get into the Rogue Gentlemen's Club take away greater knowledge and understanding of themselves. I hope they come away with a greater sense of confidence to continue in the direction that they're going, or find the track they want to be on but keep falling off. This will hopefully clear away some of the bullshit and give a firmer view of their path – and get them to walk it with more confidence.

Hotdog down a hallway
(hot-dog-down-uh-hawlway)

A wide expanse, a large opening, a loose fit, a checkered past

Common usage: *It was like throwing a hotdog down a hallway.*

FORGIVENESS

Have you ever met someone you took an instant dislike to? Yep, it saves time.

There will be people on your journey that you can't cop, whether because of your own issues or because they are just plain dickheads through and through and you can't stand a bar of them. Breathe easy, we've all been there.

Mothers-in-law get a fair hammering because they can sometimes loom large in a relationship. A mate of mine reckons his mother-in-law is a test pilot for a broom factory and says she's so bitter, she'd make a lemon tree howl. Another reckons his should be haunting a house. To be fair, I've heard quite a bit from the mothers and they too have some less than complimentary stories to tell. How could their darling daughters team up with these pigs?

It's not just the opposite sex. In some of the footy teams I've played with, you can tell the blokes who dislike each other. No amount of sitting in a circle, holding hands and singing 'Kumbaya' will fix it.

And while blokes sometimes come to blows, birds have something even more dangerous – long memories!

Someone's got to be the hero in this situation and it must be someone involved. At some stage, we need to forgive, if not for the sake of the alleged bastard who caused us this pain, then for our own peace of mind. I've read about people on their deathbed, ready to forgive and ask for forgiveness. Why wait? Tell them now. Why carry all that pain and angst all your life only to find peace at your last breath? We need to wake up.

The Honey Badger Guide to Life # 5

Forgiveness – forgive yourself and others. You don't have to forget, but forgiveness will set you free.

The people we dislike probably don't even realise how much grief they've caused us. If they did, they'd either be horrified at what they'd done or stoked they'd caused so much pain with so little effort. When you forgive from the heart, it's like a great weight has been lifted from you.

Even if you can't stand the bastard you've forgiven, you'll have the reward of no longer allowing their misdeeds to take up your valuable time.

You don't have to forget, because you don't want that same situation to occur again, but you do need to take the edge off a bad memory so it can't rattle you anymore. Forgiving someone doesn't mean you become best buds, although this can happen. It means you go about your life unburdened by a dead weight, and you can tolerate being in their presence without feeling on edge.

Take the higher ground. While it's a path less travelled, the rewards are there.

Just as you forgive others, others will forgive you. Life has a way of rewarding those who do their best. Travelling through Bosnia and Croatia a few years back, you could sense the lack of love in the camp. Those countries have a long and complicated history and forgiveness isn't high on the list of priorities. The bastards would rather fight than eat. The war back in the nineties gave each country another generation of haters and they'll be trying to settle scores for some time to come.

While we can't do much about other countries, we can start with our family, friends and relatives. We can try, and if they don't want to do the dance, well, at least we gave it a go. When your time comes to pull the pin, how good would you feel knowing that you carry no hatred from this life? It's doable.

SUCCESSFULLY ARGUING WITH YOUR PARTNER

It starts out as a lovefest. After a while, the little things start to annoy us. We usually say nothing, because we don't want to upset our beloved and on the off-chance it may risk future horizontal activity. But at some stage, we have to put the foot down and tell it like it is – bring the dark into the light, so to speak.

This is dangerous territory and, if not handled properly, it will be classed as a sneak attack, similar to a night out in Iraq.

You must first work out a battle plan.

Determining the problem

➡ Is she messy?

➡ Does she eat with her mouth open?

➡ Are her friends losers?

➡ Is she too loud/quiet?

➡ Does she bitch about others?

➡ Does she find flatulence annoying?

➡ Does she hate the thought of you riding a Shetland pony on weekends?

➡ Does she tell you that you stink?

➡ Is she holding on too tight?

While some of these may be non-standard issues, they still need to be resolved.

Setting the scene

In order to sort the show out, the environment must be non-combative. Sit your queen on the lounge and pour her a beverage. Get her something to nibble (check the expiry date). Then, out with it.

Her reaction

Women do not like being questioned or criticised, even if they're not being questioned or criticised. Her reaction to your laying it on the line will probably progress as follows:

1. An understanding smile.

2. A look of wonderment.

3. A puzzled glance.

4. A flash of hurt.

5. An icy glare.

6. A flurry of unrelated allegations.

7. Tears.

8. A slamming door.

9. Outrage.

10. No talking.

Your reaction

➤ Give her time to settle down – most women need time to process.

➤ Don't get angry or respond to drama-filled statements.

→ Under no circumstances crawl across the carpet begging for forgiveness.

→ Hold on. Things will improve.

Outcomes

After things settle down, a whole new day dawns. You should be able to communicate better and your bedroom will be filled with doves and butterflies. She may also hit you with some relevant questions, which you should answer honestly (may God have mercy on your soul).

Moving forward

→ Don't tolerate poor behaviour.

→ Don't cop yelling and screaming.

→ Don't tolerate or instigate long periods of no talkies.

→ Be kind and fair in discussions. Expect the same.

→ Be you. Don't lose your soul. If it's not going to work, then move on – it's better for both of you. If couples can learn to discuss and argue rationally, then a brilliant relationship is on the way. It's worth a shot, so look each other in the eye and go full steam ahead.

Useless as . . .

A luggage rack on a hearse

Screen doors on a submarine

A chocolate teapot

A glass door on a dunny

A third armpit

An ashtray on a motorbike

A nun at a buck's night

A pork chop at a synagogue

A roo bar on a skateboard

COURAGE

My first contact with courage was watching a western on TV with the old man. John Wayne had just defeated thousands of charging Indians, every shot a direct hit. The Duke always won the day and then he rode off with the farmer's daughter. I could never understand the fascination older people had with The Duke (or why the Indians rode in circles around a wagon train until they all got lead poisoning).

'Why is The Duke held in so much awe, Dad?' I asked. The old bloke looked at me with an understanding gaze and replied, 'Mate, The Duke fought and died in three wars, only killed the bad guys, and rode thousands, including some horses.' Well, there you have it! Thanks, Dad.

Courage comes in many forms. For some, it's just surviving, coping from day to day. For others, it's jumping out of a perfectly good aircraft, free diving, racing motorbikes or fanging around in anything with a big set of back wheels. For others, it's coping with illness – their own or someone else's.

We all face moments in life where we have to stand up. On the rugby field, players exhibit physical courage, especially when a massive South African forward hits you like a stolen truck. You bounce back up, trying to make out it was nothing, when deep down you feel like you were just cremated.

I was having a yarn to the old man about his cancer treatments and what keeps him going. 'Hope and acceptance,' he said. 'Hope that things will sort themselves out, and acceptance for the way things are.' I nodded. 'Do your best, and then go for the ride. It's that simple.' Dad related stories about sitting in the prep room while waiting for radiation treatment. He spoke of the beautiful bald women who had been through so much but were still able to smile. The quiet, reflective blokes who wondered about the future. Dad was up for his 75th radiation treatment in six years and was having a yarn to a rooster lining up for his first microwaving. 'Mate,' he said, 'don't worry about the skid mark on the bed, just be careful you don't burst into flames.' Dad also informed him that the radiation machine was called the Joan of Arc. That bloke must have thought cancer was the least of the old man's problems.

Sometimes you have to go into battle with a smile on your face. In a quiet moment, Dad told me of the tears, the sorrow and the uncontrolled emotion of those facing their own mortality. It comes to us all.

We can all be a bit selfish, and that clouds our vision of what's real. The lucky ones wake up and see the opportunities that a bad diagnosis may bring. It's a chance to look yourself in the mirror and re-evaluate, mend bridges, do good work and make up for lost time. Dad told me how much he was saving on lighting at home since the radiation treatment, and how, when the radiation machine whirs around him, he listens to Meatloaf's 'Bat out of Hell' with the volume pumped. Sanity is overrated!

When I think of courage, I can't go past my brother and sister, Joe and Lizzy, who both suffer from cystic fibrosis. In their young lives, they've battled through hundreds of hospital stays, needles, operations and drugs that smash them. Sure, it gets them down at times, but they just take a deep breath and move forward. You won't hear a word of complaint because they don't sweat the small stuff. They get it, they know what's real.

Life is about struggle, and courage shines through that struggle. Don't give up, because you don't know the half of what you can accomplish or endure. Every disappointment or failure is one step closer to your personal success. Courage will get you where you want to go.

Keep at it, champs!

TOOMPINE PUB

Some days a bloke just gets an urge. Not that one, but the urge to just get on ya bike and rack off.

An opportunity presented itself in the form of the Toompine Pub. Now, 'pub' is a pretty generous description for this joint, situated between Thargomindah and Quilpie in western Queensland. The place consists of a bar, a kitchen, a few firepits, the odd chook and some strange cats – not the animal kind.

Heaps of grey nomads in their flashed-up caravans loaded with all the mod-cons head west during the winter months, and a lot pull up stumps there for a feed and a few beers.

Russel Reid, a mate of the old man's, leases the joint and I gave him a bell to see if it was cool to drop in.

Russ is a real unit. He was once a shearer in the local area, then he moved to Brisbane to start up a bug killing business. As a young bloke, he was quite the man about town, and had been in a few blues, getting his beak bent a couple of times. He then decided he was a lover not a fighter and proceeded to have a crack at anything that moved. Hell, he'd even have a go at a shadow.

Russ was always welcoming and his answer to my question was as I expected: 'Sure, cobber, lob in.'

After a few days on the road, and a few nights under the stars, I fronted up. Those nights on your own under the twinklers really puts things in perspective.

One thing I learnt about riding out west was to pull up stumps before dusk. If you didn't follow that rule, every critter with two or more legs became a suicide bomber. Emus are the worst because they're such dumb bastards. They're just oversized sparrows with massive feathers and when you hit them, it's like hitting a pillow with a shotgun.

Anyway, when I turned up, Russ wasn't to be found. A couple of the old blokes, who were preparing a firepit for the night's bullshit stories, said he was on his way back from Quilpie with a few supplies.

Well, I was thirsty and a man is not a camel, so I hooked in. Halfway through my first beer, Russ's old ute came roaring around the corner. As it slid to a halt on the gravel, I could see the remains of a wild pig neatly wrapped around the bull bar. My first thought was Russ had started a takeaway tucker service. I didn't think it would beat pizza, but the idea had merit. Welcome to Toompine.

After rolling another couple of cans of truth serum, I had a quick tub and dropped my kit in the donga out the back. Now I had to pay for my keep. You meet some funny bastards in the outback pubs – a mixture of people who don't give a rat's arse and cow cockies worth a fortune. The thing is, you can't tell who's who.

After a few hours of selling beer and taking meal orders, I headed outside in the cold air to clear the melon.

The old stayers were sitting around the firepit, swapping stories which may or may not have been accurate.

One old rooster was going through a list of sheilas he reckoned he'd been with. Apparently, he wasn't very choosy and after looking at the outline of his scone in the fire light, you could safely say neither were the birds.

Another bloke reckoned he'd had more rides than a Melbourne Cup winner. Another still was telling all who'd listen that he'd been married three times. I couldn't help but ask him why the hell he'd put himself through it three times. He replied quietly that he loved the taste of wedding cake. The conversation went to pieces when some young bastard said John Wayne, the Duke, was a homosexual. Now, there's nothing wrong with that, but some of the old codgers took offence.

Well, enough of this fire chat for me. Russ asked me to help lock the place up and give the barflies a spray. Things were going according to plan until this old bugger refused to leave. He was well known for his inability to follow the rules, and I knew I had my work cut out. He was in his mid-sixties, weighed about 50 kilos and demanded more beer or there'd be trouble.

I couldn't help but laugh at the old fella, and told him to behave or I'd suitcase him out the door.

He replied, 'You've got a few mates have ya, ya big bastard?'

Far too funny. I shouted him another beer.

The Honey Badger Guide to Life # 6

Manners – you catch more flies with honey (Badger). Please and thank you will open many doors.

When hostilities had cooled down, we started having a yarn. He said, 'I shouldn't be drinking with what I've got.'

I said, 'What have you got?'

He said, 'About a dollar!' He got me!

Next morning, I was up at sparrow's to help in the kitchen. Some blokes in the next donga were getting ready for a shoot. I'd heard them talking about it the previous night and it sounded like they were going to kickstart World War III. A bloody gun went off about 5 metres from me, and I came close to unloading on myself – scared the hell out of me. A pig about 40 metres away went wheels up, and the boys climbed in the ute and started to drive towards it.

I yelled out, 'You mad bastard, you could've killed me.'

'But I didn't,' he said as he burned off. Fair enough.

Breakfast was a few bum nuts (eggs), bacon and some leftover goat that was hanging in the cool room. After washing it down with some black tea and snapping one off, it was time for a tub. The shower setup was a bit different. Sheets of corrugated iron for the roof and walls, and a showerhead like shrapnel damage on a Sherman tank. Halfway through the clean up, a bloody chicken pecked me on the foot. I looked up to see two of her mates coming through the half-opened door as back-up. After giving them a serve, I chased the bastards out, because I don't swing that way. The next few days were copies of the first. Chasing a horse out of the bar was a highlight. I had a bit of a wander around the joint and saw the headstones of a few camel drivers and a couple of pioneers who'd pushed it too far. It must have been a tough gig for blokes and sheilas back then. They must have had nuts the size of watermelons.

The time came to hit the road, and after a few thousand handshakes, it was time to rack off.

I roared home with a few pitstops and a victory in Broken Hill. My trusty bike did a good job for me. How shagged was I when I pulled up at home, but bloody hell, was it worth it. The people out west are a different breed, and there's always a smile and a how ya goin'. While it was a big mission, it was something I'll always remember. Always say yes to these adventures because, bloody hell, you'll enjoy it.

Carrying mud

(kareeing-mud)

Fat, winter coat, excess baggage, insulation, chubby, large, lard, tellytubby, blob

Common usage: *Let's be realistic – you're not heavy boned, you're carrying mud!*

BOYS DON'T CRY

Most of us are flat out these days. We tend to deal with our work issues but push our personal dramas to the side.

Blokes have a bad habit of not saying much about the things that really matter. It's a worry.

Breast cancer in women is a major problem, and it is constantly brought to our attention. As it should be. Yet only recently has prostate cancer been made into a big deal as a major cause of death for men. The squeaky wheel gets the oil – we have to learn from our sisters and speak up.

In the past, if a bloke spoke openly about his feelings, he was looked upon as weak. That's changing.

Women live longer than us for a few reasons, and the big one is that they talk. They get wound up, have minor freak outs and rants, then just like that, they're back! They've just taken the rubbish out.

How many times – in life, on the news or in the newspaper – do we see a bloke absolutely freak out and explode over something little?

For me, it was when I was hungry-as and my brother knew this. He wandered over and licked the last lamington. Normally, I'd give him the death stare and plot revenge. Instead, I was so full of hurt over so many things, I lost it and regretted it later.

How many blokes are so full of pain and feel that they have no way out? Can you imagine how grief-stricken some poor bastards must feel, to simply end it all?

Most of us have no idea. I hope we never will.

Blokes are a bit confused, and it's time we threw out the male behaviour books that were written too long ago. Fellas feel that they are perceived as being weak when talking about personal issues, but that's bullshit. How strong must you be to have the courage to put it all out there. Once you've aired it, you feel better, and so do your mates because you've inspired them to do the same. Like throwing a rock into a pond, the ripples are felt everywhere.

By talking about how you feel, you set yourself free. Why carry that burden of guilt, sadness, grief with you? All that weight and bullshit can only bring you down. How the hell are you going to be the best that you can be while dragging all that crap around?

I've been through tough times, just like anyone. Like you, I've built walls and hidden away. The trouble is, you can't be heard through walls and, unless you're Superman, you can't see through them either.

Brothers knock those bloody walls down. Be seen, be heard and talk. Release the emotion and feel better for it.

Some people will judge you, but only because they're not at that point of understanding yet.

Don't let other people's fears bring you down. If the people you hang around with aren't comfortable with your voyage of self-discovery, stuff 'em. You have to do what's best for you. Eventually, they will need to overcome the fear of the great unknown and find the real champion that lurks within. You can help them on their quest.

As a young footballer, I needed inspiration. I found it on Animal Planet, in the Honey Badger. I was watching this animal documentary and was amazed at just how good this little bugger was. Lions would beat the shit out of the Honey Badger, but it always got back up. Sometimes it even bit the lion on the castanets and won a famous victory. I watched this so often, and invoked it so many times on the field, the boys christened me The Honey Badger. I saw it as a name to live up to.

Take the knocks and know who you are.

Laugh, cry, and be honest with yourself. Then you'll truly know what it is to be alive.

SHORTCUMMINS

Rat with a golden tooth
(rat-widh-uh-gohlduhn-toohth)

Cunning, hidden agenda, gold-digger,
wealthy but cries poor, never shouts a round

Common usage: *When Davo told his missus
he was just gonna have a quiet one, he was
like a rat with a golden tooth.*

SHORTCUMMINS

MODERN MASCULINITY

I can't write a book called *The Honey Badger Guide to Life* and, like a country vet, not roll up my sleeves and slam the fist fair into the centre console.

So what's a modern man all about?

This is a tough question, because we're at a big crossroad. It's like standing in a giant barrel and being told to piss in the corner — a real melon scratcher.

Life for the modern bloke is busier than a one-legged man in an arse-kicking competition so let's try to navigate these dangerous waters.

I burn around the place fairly often and I've spoken to a truckload of different roosters. My conclusion: like Aussie explorers Burke and Wills, we're a bit lost. Is life simply: leave school, get a job, get married, have kids, drink, play poor golf, never speak about your feelings under any circumstances and die of a heart attack aged 59 in a freak safari accident?

A while ago the life of a male was pretty well signposted by the hairy backs that had gone before. Not today.

Too often these days, modern masculinity makes as much sense as chasing giant wheels of cheese down a steep hill or pushing butter up a porcupine's arse with a hot needle.

Too many of our mates are lost in space and totally unsure on how to act or even bloody think. We're told we're too hard or too soft; too emotional or completely unfeeling – pigs or wimps, it's a jungle out there.

Do you remember the movie *A Few Good Men*? Tom Cruise is the smart young Navy lawyer who comes out on top in a courtroom battle with Jack Nicholson (Colonel Jessup), but not before Jack gives him a dose of reality. I back Jack on that one; we need strong people who will make a stand.

The media like to elevate people for us to admire. Unfortunately, many of those cats are a mix of idiots and narcissists with little substance; not all, but some, and as media plays a big part in young lives, the problem is that these grommets see these pelicans as role models. Real heroes of the past are forgotten and clowns are elevated for us to admire. No bloody wonder we are lost.

As a rugby player with a rough melon and a decent mop, I've secured a bit of a following. Some people think I've got it all covered. While I do go after things and engage life, I still look for meaning and answers. We need to do this to improve ourselves.

As men, we're afraid to be our true selves at times for fear of what others think. We need to go about this manhood thing with greater honesty and authority about who we are and we definitely need to stop eyeing off and aspiring to adopt the lives of others.

Don't be the bloke that continuously follows. Sometimes you need to be the man that leads. Get a good grip of your tackle and form an opinion.

Be respectful of others and their thoughts and beliefs but be ruthless in your pursuit of life experience and ideas. Be yourself – because you're the best at it!

The Eight *Be's* of Modern Man

Be Polite
Manners matter. Morals have meaning. Just don't become someone else's doormat.

Be Trustworthy
The centrepiece of all relationships, be it with the finer form or friends.

Be Confident
Even if you find your strength at Friday night roller-skate discos, own yourself, son, because you're solid.

Be Excited
First, find something to get excited about. Head out and look up. Climb a tree. Get involved in life – it's seriously good and sitting out there, under the high ball, just waiting to be tackled.

Be Positive
It's too easy to bitch and whine the time away. Don't be that bloke – there's always a shard of the rainbow sitting some-where in sight. Learn to see it.

Be Courageous

Stand up for yourself. Stand up for your missus. Own an argument and don't back down from what you believe. Be strong.

Be Focused

Find whatever it is that gives you a ping of joy and zero in on it. Put in some effort and feel some reward.

Be Respectful

Listen, and let others be heard. Contemplate their opinion. Understand a woman's your equal. Not the same, but equal.

The Honey Badger Guide to Life # 7

Live now - you can't change the past, so enjoy now and aim for an even better future.

THE MAN HUG

I've been around for long enough to know the
outcome of a poor quality man hug. Let me save
you from the shrapnel of this social hand grenade.

The man hug is a serious move. It can leave someone feeling,
at best, loved or, at worst, tampered with. Are you ready for
the ramifications of this dangerous past-time?

In my old man's generation, a hug was a big move and
a rarity. Of course, dads hugged their kids when they were
young but when you were older, it was usually hands off.

Times have changed. We dish out hugs like lollies, especially when pissed.

I'm a fan of the hug. My parents, good mates and
family have to deal with it. I don't give a stuff when

or where, this self-appointed Hug Master will not be stopped. As a student of the hug, I will give you some advice regarding the joys and pitfalls associated with this phenomenon. I will also include a brief rundown of the various types beginning with the base plate of all hugs: the handshake.

From little acorns, giant oaks grow; the handshake is the pre-curser to the hug. Through history, the handshake has been a sign of greeting, honesty and strength. We can grade these as follows:

The Touch

Barely a flick of the fingers, hardly an acknowledgment.

The Dead Fish

This handshake is like two broken hands touching with fingers pointed down.

The Grasp

Used by needy people, like someone who is hanging on when drowning.

The Grab

A sign of desperation, thank God I've got you.

The Firm

Straight up and down, ridgy-didge. Solid character.

The Two-Hander

Usually used by a politician, say no more.

The Dominant

Power-hungry dickhead.

Of these, the Dominant annoys me the most. They try to pull you to them or crush your fingers as a sign of perceived strength. These people are born wankers and should be flogged with a rubber chicken. The Firm handshake is great. These people are pleased to meet you and provide solid eye-contact. You can trust these blokes.

On to the hug.

The Don't-Know-You-Well

One must be careful here. Both parties are new acquaintances and are just feeling their way. The grappling is brief and touching is minimal, if at all. Any mistakes with collision can be awkward and, if they occur, should be forgotten and forgiven immediately. Be aware of the duration – two seconds max rule.

The Bear Hug

This is to be used on a good mate or brother-in-law. You really like this bloke and probably haven't seen him for some time. He is your brother-by-another-mother. He is important to you. The hallmark of a Bear Hug is steady contact with genuine warmth. A duration of five seconds is considered reasonable.

The Blood Hug

Reserved for brothers, fathers and besties, this hug stays solid for a few seconds so the true emotion of each hugger can be transferred. This is big and can sometimes result in tears because of the raw feeling of the moment. We all need this, so don't miss the opportunity. The feeling is infectious and it spreads to others.

The Unsure Hug

When it all goes wrong . . . We have all been there. First, the clasp of hands and then you mini-step towards each other. Sometimes, we throw open our arms in preparation. Other times, we maintain the handshake and close in for a pat on the back. This is so confusing and sometimes there is accidental tackle-touching.

To avoid all these pitfalls, my advice to young punters is to practise in front of a mirror with an inflatable or imaginary friend.

You only get one shot at this, cobber: don't cock it up.

Tickler
(tikluh)

Moustache, facial hair, feather duster, pleasuring device, satisfier

Common usage: *I'm growing the tickler for Movember, you know you want it!*

EGYPT – WHY NOT?

Sometimes, all we need to drag ourselves out of a rut is a phone call.

You know the story. You're sitting on the lounge one morning, reflecting on how the party trick with the mango went bad, or you're just in a sea of poor form, and you need the dog'n'bone to start ringing.

Early October 2017 found me in a fairly shagged state. I'd been doing a heap of media stuff and felt flatter than a frisbee. Suddenly, the blower went off! It was my Uncle Mike, a fearless middle-aged competitor.

He gave me the good oil on a tour he and my old man were planning. It should have been a red flag but hell, you only live once.

Dad was in Prague, watching my brother Nath play a League Test for Norway against the Czech Republic.

His mate Russ was there as well, so all the local zoos would have been closed. They must have given the vibe of an aged and overweight Batman and Robin.

After the match, Russ was heading to Spain while Dad was meeting Uncle Mike in Israel. Their plan was to restart hostilities in the Middle East and finally get a result.

My plan was pretty simple. After the old fellas had been hurled out of the Holy Land, I'd meet them in Cairo to run a spirit-level over the pyramids. Brilliant.

The boys couldn't fly direct to Cairo from Israel, so we had to meet in Jordan first.

I think there's still a few blow-ups between the different mobs there.

The taxi to the hotel was great, if you wanted early onset lung cancer, and no amount of wheezing would give the driver a hint.

After coughing up the outrageous cab fare along with our lungs, we rocked up to our humble abode.

The hotel was cool, very flash with heaps of well-dressed staff who smiled a lot. None of them could speak reasonable English and my Arabic wasn't that good, so things seemed to edge downhill.

While going through the entry, the alarm went off big time.

For reasons unknown, the old man had bought a bayonet in Prague (who does that?) and the scanner had picked it up.

The staff politely indicated they would keep it till he left and it seems this was where the mutual mistrust began.

Dad didn't help matters when he threatened to use it on the next bastard who tried to sell him something.

That night, we tucked into a feed that tasted a bit like goat on toast.

For entertainment, we listened to an Egyptian bird sing about an Egyptian bloke who gave her a fig for her birthday.

After a few beers that smelt suspiciously like camel urine, we moved onto the safety of shiraz, and planned our assault on Tutankhamun's holiday home.

There's a fair bit of Badger history around these parts.

My great-grandfather, William Gerald Cummins, trained next to the pyramids in 1915.

He had joined the 9th Light Horse and landed at Gallipoli as a trooper.

In his letters home, he didn't give the locals a big rap. He claimed that if he stood still long enough, they'd steal his shadow.

My great-uncle, Dick Sweeny, parked his arse there as well during World War II.

He wasn't fussed on the blokes, but he did want to bring a couple of sheilas home to the farm after he cleaned up the Italians in Libya.

He reckoned two would be enough: one bird in full kit to cook and do the housework, and a good sort to do the dance of a thousand veils around the cot.

It didn't work out too well because they shipped the poor bastard to New Guinea to stop the Japanese setting up camp.

Now, back to our mission.

Our plan was to meet with the head rooster at the front desk early next morning. We'd met him on our arrival and immediately christened him Gecko. Every time we asked the poor bastard a question, his eyes bulged to the size of beach balls. It reminded me of being in Year 4. Best three years of my life.

The next morning, after a swim, a feed and swiftly snapping one off, we were ready for action.

Uncle Mike started negotiations with Gecko but was sacked after confusing everyone.

Dad was also made redundant after his opening spray, in which he referred to his bayonet. It was my time to shine.

We decided on a car to pick us up at the hotel and take us to Giza to check out the rock triangles. We'd burn around these for a couple of hours, take a few happy snaps and rack off – too easy.

The driver was happy enough, but we already suspected the evil that lurked behind that seven-tooth smile.

After fifteen minutes, an interpreter jumped into the cab and informed us that for a small fee, we could hear about the history of Egypt.

'Off' was the second word he got from Dad as he leapt from the car at the next set of lights.

Second stop was a genuine papyrus reed shop, where we were encouraged to make a boat from the papyrus and then buy it.

Uncle Mike was filthy, offering to make a papyrus coffin and bury the bastard in it.

We climbed back into the cab and the old man read the riot act, telling our seven-tooth wonder that he and his livestock were in serious danger of being interfered with if he didn't take us to the famous pile of rocks, pronto.

Victory. We rocked up to the three pyramids and the Great Sphinx and were blown away.

How the pharaohs and the labour unions came to work out agreements over this is a wonder to all building companies.

Trying to get photos without being harassed was a bloody mission.

They just won't leave you alone until you buy a rubber pyramid. Uncle Mike informed one young kid with legs like an ibis that he would find the rubber pyramid jammed up his arse, while the old man threatened to club him to death with the tail bone of a Hittite.

It seemed to work, as he wandered off, wishing us well in Arabic and gestured there was only one hour till closing time.

The trip back to the hotel was uneventful, except when the driver decided to take a shortcut. He was met with a chorus of 'NO, PRICK, NO' until he reset course.

We left the cab at the hotel, giving the driver a small tip and suggesting he not breed.

That night at dinner, we discussed the day and thought up some new insults. While we had more adventures ahead of us, that day was a cracker.

After the feed, we disputed the thievery allowance at the bottom of the bill while the old man informed the waiter that Cleopatra had a nice arse.

We left that day on a high.

These memories are great.

Take the time to say yes. You'll never regret it.

FUNEMPLOYMENT

We get all sorts at my Rogue Gentleman weekends.

Most are blokes who are a bit lost. They're looking for something personally and professionally, a direction and a purpose. They know they're capable of more – as workers, friends, partners and individuals.

Often they're great men who have lost good jobs.

Like the cross-eyed teacher I know who got fired because he couldn't control his pupils.

Or the student of Russian philosophy who dropped out of Communism class because of rotten Marx.

Or the bloke I met who threw away his career because that fella was addicted to brake fluid . . . I wasn't worried about him – he told me he could stop at any time.

BEARDED MACADAMIAS

We all have a mate who is a bit different from the rest. But my mate was the kind of bloke I could rely on . . . for entertainment that is. To protect his identity, I'll call him Kent. Kent once ate an entire carton of eggs 'cause he lost a bet. Not sure why he ate the shells, though. But that's the content of this bloke's character – puts his own health at risk to impress the lads. And I was impressed.

So we packed our bags and got ready for a bloke's weekend camping on an island near Airlie Beach. I loaded my bag with all the essentials. I asked Kent what was in his bag as it looked excessively large for a weekend away. The contents of his bag looked something like this:

→ Three singas

→ Three strides

→ Two G-bangers (one black, one leopard print)

→ Two jumbo boxes of dingers

→ One busted arse toothbrush.

It doesn't sound like much, but throw in a fold-out tantra chair and the old duffle bag was maxed out.

So we boarded our chariot 'Battle Cat', a barely roadworthy dark green Suzuki Swift with only three good wheels. I got it serviced before we left, and by serviced, I mean we kicked the tyres and got a retired brickie to look under the hood. Just to be on the safe side. The advice I was given post-inspection was, 'Take a fire extinguisher with ya, she looks angry!'

So with all the safety checks done and dusted, we hit the road with our trusty steed. If we weren't overloaded we probably would've taken Bluey, my dad's goat. It's amazing how much space a BBQ, a surfboard and a few duffle bags can take up . . .

We blazed a trail up the coast with borrowed cash, high hopes and charismatic wit. In spite of the non-serviced loans, empty bank accounts, an overheating vehicle and one day's rations, we were free. Though I'm sure that this was just another day for Kent. 'It's good to chance ya arm every so often,' I thought, reassuring myself more than anything else.

We parked at the marina and rocked up to board the vessel, knowing that the Battle Cat wasn't worth stealing and it was the right decision to leave the doors unlocked to give a would-be thief a good look around to come to the same conclusion. Wearing our best pairs of double pluggers, we wanted to look flash. We landed on the island with a few cans in us to take the edge off, and we were met with a warm reception by a few fit-looking birds. Seagulls, I think they were . . .

We set up the swags and went over the battle plan for the day/night's proceedings. No beers until 10 am and bro before . . . We were all set. By 11:05 am, security politely moved us on from our first watering hole, something to do with running out of soft drink I'd say.

After that, we lost track of time, we were having so much fun. One pub to the next; Tinder is so much more time effective these days. We met some lovely young felines at this one pub called 'Shag on a Rock'. It seemed like it was going to live up to its name when out of nowhere Kent decides it's time for us to do a nudie run. He got out what looked like a bee sting and a pair of bearded macadamia nuts. Our lives flashed before our eyes when, for some reason, security took Kent for a walk. It was a bit strange 'cause there was nothing to look at where they took him, it was dark behind those industrial bins. I didn't want to leave a mate hanging, so to speak, so I headed towards them in my birthday suit. Who would've thought two security guards were up for nude tackling practice? Still not sure who was tackling who though.

Still in the nude, we were soon heading back towards our swags when Kent decided to roll over a golf buggy into the water. I think he still had some energy to burn off. Then suddenly, talk about coincidence, those security guards were back; this time they had a few mates that wanted to play. They must have heard how much fun we had the first time.

I thought it would be a good time to see what was on the other side of the island, so I fired up another golf buggy and off we went. It was pretty funny, Kent had climbed on top of the buggy and was holding on like a spider monkey. Four security guards in tow, I felt like a nude Indiana Jones.

We made it, what a buzz! Kent even got a free ride out by the Water Rats. What a great service, they even took him back to the station for a guided tour. Some minor paperwork/admin at the Mackay Police Station and we were on our way home. What a tour!

Dingle berries
(dingguhl-berees)

Balls, testes, dugs, canisters, clackers, nuts, doggie bag, cods, beanbag, pills

Common usage: *That gelding kicked me in the dingle berries.*

THE CHUB HOTEL

There was a quiet little watering hole that supported the mighty Buckin' Turtles rugby team. It wasn't the flashiest joint, but it seemed to attract the sort of company that you would see in a *Star Wars* film. In fact, I remember a regular drinking his amber lemonade through what appeared to be a snout. There were some unique humans, to say the least. But every one of them would always make you feel very welcome.

We finished our usual Saturday rugby match with the team victory song. This usually involved every member of the club, the players, their relatives, the cuz's bros, their next-door neighbours, two dogs, a cat and a dozen cartons in one dressing shed, with one working shower and a seat-less thunder box that wouldn't flush. We wouldn't have had it any other way.

Like the Israelites' mass exodus from Egypt, we made a beeline to the Chub to galvanise our steely victory. We liked to just ease into it . . . well, until the Chub manager decided payment was optional. It was like happy hour on steroids, the bartender ended up with a repetitive strain injury (RSI) and did the noble thing, letting us help ourselves. Within twenty minutes, I remember Luke behind the bar with his back to us, two hands in the fridge, throwing black rats over his shoulders like a food drop for survivors of a natural disaster. It was relentless. I have never seen a bloke empty a fridge with no trace of the evidence in such a short period of time.

Needless to say, it was an eventful night with a few scuffles, a dozen hook-ups, two arrests, a restraining order, a marriage proposal and some pending investigations. It was one of our quieter weekends. Mind you, it was all considered good fun and the local law enforcement, to their credit, requested two weeks' notice before our next gathering. We had a lot of respect for them, they kept things in order and fully understood the need to celebrate.

One day when they were busy with their normal duties upholding the law, a call came through that a crime was taking place. Without hesitation like Starsky and Hutch, a few of the Johnnies charged into the hot zone (a house party gone wrong). Me and a few of the lads were at a

BBQ a few doors down when it all went pear-shaped. We wandered out the front, thinking the night's entertainment had arrived, only to see what looked like *Gladiator* meets *Braveheart*. Shirtless blokes with face paint wielding fence palings, skirmishes breaking out across the street, animals running past, scattered spot fires from ill-directed fire-crackers flaring up. It was pretty wild.

After we finished our cans, we thought it best to approach with caution and try to ease the situation. That idea vanished in an instant when Disco Stu (a good mate of ours) got caught up in the excitement, launched in and nailed someone. As in nature, turtles flock together. In what could have been described as a V-formation we swooped in with military precision. It's hard to say how much we really helped, given the amount of property damage, missing animals and human injury, but I think we made a difference . . .

Not stupid, simply . . .

Dumb as a stump

Not the full quid

Thick as a brick

A shingle short of a roof

A few bricks short of a load

A few Tim Tams light of a packet

A few bites short of a bikkie

A few bangers shy of a barbie

Not the sharpest tool in the shed

The lift doesn't go all the way
to the top

Shit-for-brains

Nits in the network

If brains were dynamite, he
couldn't blow his hat off

Bright as a two-watt globe

Got space to sell between
the ears

A few pies short of a grand final

So brainless he'd pick his nose
and his head would cave in

A few white ants in the woodwork

A few palings short of a fence

So slow he couldn't get a job
as a speed bump

Only one oar in the water

Wouldn't know his arse from
his elbow

THE GROG TALKING

I get why blokes hook into the truth serum. It's legal for a start, and it's great to have a couple and a yarn with some good mates.

I've rarely had a skinful but when I have, I've paid for it the next day.

In footy, team bonding was always a big one. We didn't hit it often because grog slows you down. Being a well-oiled team is good, but not too well-oiled.

Seeing life through a set of beer goggles can briefly lift your spirits. But some roosters use the booze as a crutch. If you need to be as full as a doctor's wallet every day, you need help, you poor bastard.

Grog can bring out the best and the worst in us. After a few scoops, some blokes see themselves as chick magnets. Some become knowledgeable on all topics. Others feel that only kryptonite jammed up their arse will stop them.

Unfortunately, on the dark side, it can be the fuse that makes blokes want to pick more fights than North Korea.

Having a background in sport, I've had to be careful not to overdo it with the happy water. It can be a little bit of a beast, and I've seen weird acts and poor form associated with overindulgence.

Once you've said or done something, whether you meant it or not, you can't reverse it.

One good mate of mine regained consciousness one morning only to find a large W tattooed on each arse cheek. He refers to it as his 'WOW' tat.

My grandfather Bill Cummins didn't mind a refreshing ale on a hot day. Back in the 70s, he had a business transporting grain from the KB Brewery near Lismore and selling it to the local farmers.

One day, he was called to collect 10,000 cans of beer and take them to the tip. That's like putting Dracula in charge of the blood bank. Apparently, the alcohol content was too high, so they couldn't legally sell them. On his way to the tip, he diverted to his industrial sheds, called all his mates and upended the booze onto the concrete floor.

The food in the smoko fridge found itself in the bin and the fridge was now jam-packed with over-strength conversation starters. After a few hours of loyal commitment, the boys were as full as the last bus. Many great songs were butchered that afternoon.

Early the next day, the boys rocked up to help Grandad move the clothesline and cut down a large tree. Grandma was at the window, giving him some safety advice, as she'd seen old Billy in action and expected the worst.

I gazed in wonderment as Billy downed a couple of cans before he dispatched the tree. As the large gum smashed into the roof, it seemed a bit like slow-motion. When it rolled off the guttering onto the previously relocated clothesline, things seemed to pick up pace. Grandma tried to scream but no words came out. I left as she was furiously looking up the Yellow Pages for a euthanasia clinic. I dunno why. Surely there was a case for justifiable homicide.

The Honey Badger Guide to Life # 8

Accept blame – own what you've done, accept you've ballsed it up at times and move on.

So inebriated as to be . . .

Stonkered	Full as a doctor's wallet
Shickered	Full as a sumo's sock
Zonked	Up to pussy's bow
Tanked	Lit up like a Christmas tree
Blotto	Rotten as a chop
Pissed as a newt	Loaded
Pissed as a parrot	High as a dingo's howl
Full as a bull's bum	Shot full of holes
Drunk as a skunk	Three sheets to the wind
Full as the last bus	

SPIRITUALITY – HOW TO PRAY

Did you hear about the dyslexic, agnostic insomniac? He lay awake all night, wondering if there was a dog!

Think about it.

I'm not a religious person, but I am a spiritual rooster. I did the altar-boy thing and was a churchgoer while growing up at home. Altar wine was much sought-after when backs were turned. Helping out at wedding ceremonies was always something to look forward to. Everyone was happy and the groom's wallet was usually open.

My brothers Luke and Nathan were old hands at it. Ring the bloody bells on time and smile. What groom wouldn't want to give five dollars to a happy blond-haired altar boy in full kit? Those were the days.

During the days when the family went to church, we learnt to pray the standard way – *Our Fathers*, etc. Pretty straightforward.

Confession was a tough one. As a kid, we were obliged to go once a month to keep us on track. Whatever evil you'd perpetrated on earth had to be told to a man in a robe who knew you. How embarrassing! Once, when I was about thirteen, I told the priest I was having thoughts about a girl in my class. He named a few of the girls but I wouldn't tell him who I was keen on. He did, however, give me some good leads on how to stay on the straight and narrow.

For penance, he gave me a thousand *Hail Marys* and an act of contrition. I couldn't for the life of me work out why God would want me to repeat the same words over and over. Still, who am I to question Christianity?

I'm sure hell couldn't handle me, and I'm not that sure heaven wants me.

These days, I still pray, because I believe there is a supreme entity. Whether you believe in God, Buddha, Allah, Jehovah, Vishnu, Gandhi, John Wayne, or whatever, it doesn't matter.

If good comes from what you believe in, it's the one for you.

A lot of people these days have moved away from mainstream religions for various reasons. Humans seem to have complicated religion to the point where people lose interest.

We need to take a step back, settle down and get back to the basics.

On some of my bike trips, I find myself alone and sitting under the stars. I usually have a yarn to the big fella upstairs and tell him my plans. I'm sure I can hear him laughing.

Talk to your God in a way you would talk to a loved one, trusted friend or someone you respect. Someone is listening to you, so bare your soul. It's good for us and helps us to cut through all the layers of bullshit in this world.

**The Honey Badger
Guide to Life # 9**

Tell the truth – it's much easier than
thinking up a lie and trying
to remember it.

FISHIN' IN THE NORTHERN TERRITORY

Not long after the wet season had ended in the Northern Territory, my brother Luke asked if the old man and I wanted to go fishing. It was a done deal. I was on the next flight up, keen as mustard to bag 'em, tag 'em, flip 'em and spin 'em with my new rod and reel. After the eagle had landed, I felt the heatwave that is Darwin. A mild 36 degrees, and what felt like a billion per cent humidity. While waiting for an evac outside the airport, I met a friendly local lad who gave me what seemed to be a compliment.

'Aye brudda, you got a thick neck . . . Can I have a dollar?'

'Na, I'm out of brass, mate. Do you want a fiver instead?'

'Na, just a dollar!'

Now there is a man who had principle and was not prepared to settle for anything other than what he wanted. I admire that.

The Honey Badger Guide to Life # 10

Happiness - it's in you. No amount of brass or possessions, birds or blokes, will make you totally happy. It's a conscious decision - make it!

My brother turned up in the Toyota Hilux and yelled 'Hey Badge, get in!' We were on our way with rods and reels on standby, a tackle box full of lures and a jumbo packet of chips. Our first stop was to flick off the drains and try to jag ourselves a monster. The run off is a good time to go, 'cause the barra lie and wait, near the drains. We hooked a few tarpons, which boosted our morale and launched us onto the next spot.

The sun was about to turn in for the day when we rocked up to some swampy wetlands. I saw what looked like a big log in the water. It was no log – it was a 4.5 metre croc. After having a good look at us, it slowly sank below the surface, barely leaving a ripple. We walked about ten paces further and started fishing. It's incredible how much water flows through this place. It was something out of Nat Geo, with the sun setting, wild buffalo grazing on the bank, red-tailed black cockatoos making the sounds of something prehistoric on the afternoon breeze. A squadron of mosquitoes had gathered and landed on me with a thud, big hungry bastards. We sprayed the bastards just before we needed a blood transfusion, caught enough fish for a feed, rounded out the day, and headed for home. We stopped for a night cap at the Humpty Doo Tavern and met a mob of locals, which gave us a reason to have a few extras.

There's nothing better than downing a couple with some characters. This place was a good mix of champions and aliens and they all had stories to tell.

Even though we were a bit peckish, the tucker in the pie-warmer was a sad story. It resembled the leftovers from an early explorer's ration pack. Even the flies wouldn't land on it.

The highlight of the trip was talking to a bloke who had his own face tattooed on the back of his hand. After a quick yarn with that trend-setter, we were out of there.

Holdin' on like a hair on a biscuit

(hohldin-on-luyk-uh-hair-on-uh-biskuht)

To cling on for dear life, hold tight, be a pest, immoveable

Common usage: *I was punching well above my weight and holdin' on like a hair on a biscuit.*

ROGUE CHAMPIONS

Reg 'Snowy' Baker

Have you ever had the urge to wear your grunders on the outside, a beach towel flowing cape-like from your shoulders, as a group of nude Nigerian weightlifters holds you aloft?

No? Good, that would be unnatural.

Very few reach the dizzy heights where they are admired and adored as a superhero. The closest I came was after the 2008 Hong Kong Sevens, when I was at a bang-up do and this pissed giant in a Superman suit threatened to jam kryptonite up my arse.

But let's talk about Snowy.

Snowy Baker was Australia's greatest all-round athlete. If I was burning a couple of steaks and could invite some winners over, I'd cooee that bugger in a flash.

'Hey Snowy, ya weak bastard, drag your arse out here and wrap your laughing gear around my newest cremation!'

Snowy played and excelled at 26 different sports. At eighteen, he was the national middleweight and heavy-weight boxing champion. Snowy also represented in rugby union, hockey, rowing, fencing, water polo, cricket and surfing.

In 1908, he was selected to compete at the London Olympics in swimming, diving and boxing, the only time an athlete has represented in three different sports at the same Olympics.

Once Snowy conquered a sport, he would move on and find another hill to climb.

His answer to everything seemed to be, bugger it, why not?

Now I've been to a few dos during my rugby days, and I've had a couple of chinwags with some real winners.

The thing they all have in common is that 'grab it with both hands' attitude – just like Snowy.

It's history that Snowy was rolled in the Olympic boxing final by a Pommy called Douglas. The legend is another story.

It's said that the referee for that fight was Douglas's father, and even though Douglas was bashed around the ring in a fashion similar to a late night at Sleaze Ball, he was crowned the winner.

Snowy accepted the result with dignity but two nights later, both boxers and their friends were feasting at a flash joint in London.

I'm not sure what was said or how it started, but both fellas ripped in and began belting the tripe out of each other in the middle of the restaurant. Snowy dropped him, had a few beers and finished his feed. I imagine he would have called out, 'Now someone clean that shit up.'

His work as a sportsman was done. What's next?

Snowy became Australia's leading actor and starred in a dozen movies, including such box office smashes as *The Man from Kangaroo* and *Shadow of Lightning Ridge*.

Like most good things Australia has to offer, someone else wanted him. Snowy hit the road and opened a ranch in

California. He taught horse riding, fencing and swimming to Hollywood stars like Elizabeth Taylor and Rudolph Valentino.

Snowy Baker – one of the greats, and another Rogue Champion.

BADGERSAURUS

Beer. AKA...

Amber fluid

Neck nectar

Gullet oil

Idiot juice

Brown biscuits

Malt sandwiches

Truth serum

Happy water

Frosty chops

Snake juice

Lunatic soup

BADGERSAURUS

TAKING THE PISS

After a storm in the Bass Strait, two Queensland sailors, Macca and Donk, find themselves adrift.

As the storm clears, Donk takes charge: 'Righto, the first thing we need to do is check the lifeboat top-to-bottom to see what supplies are on board.'

While scrambling around, looking for food, water and flares, Macca finds an old lamp.

Well what else could you do? Macca rubs the lamp and sure enough a bloody genie pops out.

You know the drill. The genie tells these blokes he'll grant them any wish they desire.

Before Donk can say 'Rescue helicopter', Macca opens his big yap and blurts out: 'Turn the ocean into XXXX!'

The genie claps his hands and immediately Bass Strait turns into a vast ocean of golden beer.

The genie disappears and Macca, who's dry as a dead dingo's doolacky after a morning in the sun, sticks his head over the side of the boat and guzzles up as much amber fluid as he can.

Not only does the ocean of beer taste great, it's also as cold as a mother-in-law's kiss.

It's only when Macca finally surfaces that he sees Donk is mad as a cut snake.

'What's up, Donk? Surely an ocean of XXXX is every Queensland bloke's dream come true.'

'Yeah,' says Donk, 'but now we're gonna have to piss in the boat.'

THE AUSSIE LARRIKIN

What happened to the Aussie way? What happened to the Aussie sense of larrikinism? What happened to holding an opinion and not running scared of causing offence? What is this outrage culture that's come to question everything and everyone?

Don't get me wrong: you can't go around deliberately insulting people or discriminating against anyone or causing harm. Let's get that clear from the kick off. But I've had a gutful of the constant PC bullshit. The fear that so many people live in these days of saying what they want to say, thinking the way they want to think without being bloody jumped all over and scrutinised to death. Enough.

Playing rugby – there was always a bit of heat. You'd get whacked. You'd whack back. You'd get opened up and spill some claret. You'd return fire. But then, at the end of the game, you'd shake hands, move on, and then go and share a bloody beer together.

The way I see it, we need to get to that point ASAP. Instead of going, 'Oh, you bastards,' right off the bat, why don't we just get over it and be like, 'I don't agree with you, but I'm not going to set fire to your Shetland pony to make a point.'

I don't agree with a lot of what's being sprayed about the world, but I don't have to be offended by it or take it to heart. People are entitled to their views – but no one has to give those views the time of day if they don't want to. And why the hell would we all want to be in a world without differ-ence? That would be bloody boring, for starters.

This stuff shits me because it's not what we're about as Australians. At least, it's not what we used to be about, or what we pride ourselves on being about. We were always a bunch who wanted to get on with each other, who welcomed each other and who looked out for each other even when we didn't always agree. I mean, that's what mateship comes down to in my book, and I love the idea that as Aussies we all hold each other as mates no matter what our back-grounds or jobs or languages or gender or whatever. But things have crossed a line – we've unlinked those hands and instead of using hands to give someone a leg up we're using them to strangle the poor bastard. What. The.

I get over to New Zealand a bit and those fellas are always taking the piss out of me and out of me being an Aussie. You know, 'You root kangaroos' and that carry-on. It's not some of their best lines but I always reply, 'Yeah, but I always make a second date.' Now, if I was a card-carrying VIP member of the bloody outrage club then I'd be calling them out as racists. As pigs. And I'd be causing grief to someone – to their self-worth, family or career – by doing it.

But instead, I get the sense of jest they intend, I don't get offended and we all move along together. The end.

And this is my point: it's about having a laugh, not taking stuff too seriously, seeing the light-heartedness, the larrikin-ism, that was intended in the first place.

A couple of years back I got into some drama for my language in one of the Tradie undie ads. Yep – a massive shit fight flared up because I'd referred to them as 'the duck's nuts'. People complained to the bloody Advertising Standards Bureau – letters were sent in and emails pinged off. There was a hearing into the use of my language – whether it was appropriate or whether it was obscene, as claimed by those who'd got their knickers all twisted up about it.

It kind of makes me laugh when I think about this panel going about an official investigation into the use of the term 'the duck's nuts'. I mean, 'the duck's nuts'? These undies *are* the duck's nuts — they should have bloody praised me for some actual honesty in advertising instead of forming an anti-duck's nuts panel.

In the end, the Bureau found that while I was speaking about a duck's nuts — its balls, its testicles — it didn't think the language was 'strong or obscene or inappropriate in the circumstances'.

I laughed about the situation. And then I got riled up about it too. Was it really necessary to pour all that time, energy and money into an investigation about that? You'll have your own opinion, but I don't think so. And there've been other bits and pieces I've been forced to cut out of some of my other ads and work, because some people thought other people might object. Yep, people getting upset about what other people might or might not get upset about. How the hell did we get here?!

As I see it, we need to start questioning all the offence and the offended. It's a fine line, because if you do become that person, then everyone jumps to the conclusion that you're saying it's okay to be a racist or a sexist or an un-PC type or whatever. Absolutely not, and you should call that shit out, no question. I think it's just about sometimes saying, a joke is just a joke. Sometimes you can be a bit cheeky, be a larrikin, and that's all it is.

I was talking to my old man about this. We were saying there's two ways to come at it.

First, you can fight back like that, call out the offended, live your life and not worry about the fallout. You'll get a lot of haters and cop a heap of shit, but some people will agree with you.

And the other way is to clearly withdraw from it and wait for things to come full circle. I reckon more and more people will come to realise that our wellbeing and our way of life is eroded when we are always being offended or being worried about possibly offending others, or even being offended on behalf of someone who isn't actually offended.

Because I'll say this – I think our quality of life has been diminished as a result of all of this. We can't say anything. We can't do anything. We can't wear anything. Everything might upset this person or that person. Life's not fun anymore.

But people will get to this point, and then there'll be a bloody revolution. And all of a sudden, we'll be back to the way things should be.

I bloody hope so anyway.

MY DEADSET WAY OF TALKING

I got noticed as much for the things I was saying off the footy field as how I played on it. Yep – The Badger became a force because I spoke like so many Aussies no longer do.

And I'm proud of that. I'm proud to be a bloke putting it out there.

A lot of people reckon it's put on – that it's all fake and that I play up for the cameras. And that's fine – they've never met me and that's just their opinion. See – not offended!

But generally they meet me and they realise this is me – it's just who I am. I'm an Aussie – if you want to put a label on it. And that's sweet. Because there's something great about being an Aussie — at our core we're about not walking straight lines but being a maverick, a character; we buck trends and question what people see as normal. And best of all, they go about things with a sense of bloody humour! That's what makes us unique.

It stems from the tough times — and I mean the proper tough times, not just the morning your barista hands you a full-milk flat white instead of your usual skinny cap.

In the tough times — be it the Depression, the Gold Rush or the Changi POW camps, or whenever Australia has been going through some sour personal shit — well, it's been about finding a laugh where possible. And the real Aussie is that person — the one who comes out and drops some bloody Australian vernacular, some funny Australian witticism, and then all of a sudden people are having a laugh. It's infectious, that laughter, and people want to get on board with it. It brings us Aussies together, it overcomes our differences, and when that laughter comes, it changes the energy.

I copped my way of talking from being around my brothers, my dad, my family. We'd be sitting around the dinner table or in the shed and talking like this — we had all these sayings. And I thought, 'Why are we holding this back?' I just think it's such an important part of us, as Australians.

It's probably no little surprise to hear that I failed my media training when playing rugby. I just didn't understand why they wanted us to speak like robots all the time.

And so instead of listening to them I'd always remember what Dad told me – 'If you don't know what to say, just tell 'em a story like what you did on your holidays.' So that's what I did – and then suddenly, lo and behold, the interviewer would be more interested in what I was telling them than the answer to the question he'd asked anyway. And then it would be on the internet and all of a sudden I'd have a million-plus views.

People responded to it – they'd stop me and thank me for the way I was talking, for bringing some fun back and also for not shying away from being Aussie. For me it's about being honest and true to who I am. It's also about being authentic to Australia, to the best parts of our culture and an identity that we seem to be fast forgetting. Not on my watch.

RUM MATHEMATICS

I figured that, as a local team in Bundaberg, we should probably be able to get a few free bottles of Bundy Rum for the boys. So I picked up the phone, put it on speaker and gingerly asked the brewery if they could throw us a bone and share some grog.

After a short silence, the bloke on the other end of the tin cup replied, 'Yeah, we have a few pallets of leftover promotional premix you can have, if you want?'

Well, we almost had an orgasm. 'Yeah, thanks, Davo, it will probably get us through the weekend,' I replied as calmly as possible, not to give off any hint of how bloody chuffed we were. 'The drama is, I have nowhere to store it and it needs to be shared with other clubs.' Without hesitation, my brother Luke replied, 'No dramas, there's an old warehouse just down the road and we can distribute the goods from there. I'll send over the flatbed eight tonner this arvo and we'll get rid of them for ya.'

We convinced the driver at Luke's workplace to take an extended lunch break while we put a few clicks on the old girl. We were inbound, destination: Bundaberg Rum Factory. We convinced ourselves she could carry about twelve tonnes if she had to, and swore an oath not to sample any delights until the goods were disseminated to the shareholders (rugby clubs). We turned up just on dusk, ready to close out the deal with an intent of high morality and a criminal's wit. True to his word, Davo landed two pallets (88 cartons) of some of the finest (not far past its use-by date) premix rum and cola on the eastern seaboard. Geez, it felt good. We drove out of there like Lawrence of Arabia and his donkey and took a direct path to the warehouse. We broke a cold sweat each time we had to stop at a red light or give way, because if those Bundy lads got one whiff of the top-secret haul we had on board, it would be like something out of *Black Hawk Down*.

We made it. The stash was in lockdown, and it was time to do the noble thing and call the rugby clubs so they could come and get their share of the spoils. One club was suffering financial difficulty and couldn't front the cash so, in the eyes of Rum Law, they had to be overlooked. That left us with four clubs. The date and time were set for the extraction. The first club turned up with a box trailer.

Luke: 'Well you won't be needing that.'

Meathead: 'What do you mean? There's 88 cartons divided by five, that's 17.6 cartons each!'

Luke: 'Well, have you heard of inflation and GST?'

Meathead: 'Yeah, so?'

Luke: 'Well, that's got nothing to do with us, but what I can say is that, in the name of equal rights and responsible service of alcohol, some sacrifices had to be made.'

At this moment, the other club representatives had just rolled up and they looked thirsty. I softly closed the warehouse doors to keep the merchandise from prying eyes, in case of a Chernobyl-type meltdown.

Luke: 'Ah, right on time, welcome fellas!'

Rissole: 'Hey, Cummins, we're here for our four cartons.'

Thomo: 'Yeah, me too.'

Meathead: 'Four cartons? Shouldn't it be seventeen?'

Luke: 'I'm glad you other blokes have done the maths correctly. Twenty cartons divided by four, less a few transport damages, warehouse rent, fuel and wear and tear on the 20 tonner and market volatility, equals 3.6666 cartons each. Let's call it four and be done with it. Now where would you like your four cartons?'

Meathead: 'Back seat.'

Rissole: 'Same here.'

Thomo: 'Same.'

This one deal alone kept our club afloat for another season. The rugby gods smiled on us that day, and well into the future, thanks to the other clubs and supporters purchasing our premix (with a scratch mark where the use-by date should be) from our canteen for the next three seasons . . .

We did the right thing and I doubt a court in the land would have frowned on our efforts.

TIMBUKTU

The Aussie poetry championships were taking place. There were two finalists, a bloke from the University of NSW and a country bumpkin from the outback. They were given twenty seconds to come up with a poem about Timbuktu. Up first was the uni student . . .

'On the lonely desert sands crossed a lonely caravan, men on camels two by two. Destination: Timbuktu.' The crowd cheered.

Then the bloke from the outback stood up. 'Tim and I off hunting went, found three girls in a pop-up tent. They were three and we were two, so I bucked one, and Tim bucked two!'

Dinger
(dinguh)

Condom, tarp, anti-child support device, lion tamer, sleeping bag, goat skin

Common usage: *If it's not on . . . it's not on! Use a dinger.*

THE BADGER'S GUIDE TO THE BEDROOM

Most young blokes are constantly thinking about doing the wild thing. It's what gets them up in the morning and stops them rolling out of bed at night.

Some fellas like fellas, and that's fine. If you're a fan of the two-man wheelbarrow race, without the wheelbarrow, fair enough. It's not my cup of tea, but as they say, 'if you've got balls, roll,' so whatever floats your boat.

Bad sex, good sex

Let's drop our tackle on the table and talk, eye to eye. Hang onto your G-string as we discuss a few home truths.

The bedroom comes in more shapes and flavours than a Paddle Pop.

Back in the day, if a young bloke played hide the sausage, he would tell his mates ASAP. It was a big deal because, as the saying goes, if you boned 'em, you owned 'em.

These days, the birds chase just as much as the blokes.

Scented candles, Batman suits, handcuffs and semi-trailer-loads of Viagra are all part of today's mating rituals. It can be wild, calm, good or great. Just don't get your weaponry caught in the zipper.

As a young rooster, the very sight of a nude sheila puts you in a tailspin. You have visions of yourself as a sexual tractor, ploughing ripened fields, but there's more to it. Way back when, the boys would do their best and be happy with it. Today, women expect a little more. Hell, a lot more.

Here's a few hot tips . . .

➤ Check all bedroom cupboards to avoid a surprise visit from a Wonder Woman impersonator who wants to flog you with a wet shoelace.

➤ Remember, you're not driving at Bathurst. Too much speed can create friction, which may result in spontaneous combustion. Try explaining that to the coppers!

➤ Sometimes, it doesn't have to be about fireworks. People need to be held close, to feel safe. Birds can act a little tough, but deep down, most just want someone to love them.

The early finisher

It happens to most blokes at some stage. You're that keen to party at pleasuredom that the party is over before it begins. There are a few theories about hanging on. A mate of mine reckons that when the wolf is at the door, he just thinks of his mother-in-law. That solves the issue quick!

Tackle

Most tackle is usually about the same dimensions. Just as some birds have hooters that block out the sun, some blokes could pole-vault to the next suburb with their particular jack hammers.

We mortals have to do the best with what we've got. If you've got bugger-all, focus on improving your technique.

All said and done, it's not what you've got, it's how you use it. Do your best.

Bedroom talk

Yelling and screaming like you're caught in a barbed-wire fence may be cool at first, but ideally you want to build up to the fireworks.

A few words on your partner's finer points usually gets the show started. Getting your gear off followed by a meaningful squirrel grip will get the dance underway.

A word of warning – never call out your own name followed by 'go, you good thing'. It's a rookie error.

Happy humping.

hat the shuck? Spearing a few oysters down in Smoky Bay.

The Badge on The Bridge. Doing a live cross to the *Today* show from the top of the Coathanger.

Emus have the worst road sense – run into one of those and it's like hitting a pillow with a shotgun.

Losing my shirt at Lake Eyre, 15 metres below sea level but not a drop in sight.

Sunset at the Great Australian Bight.

The door's always open, folks. All you've got to do is knock.

Margaret River – great wine, super sunsets, top surf. Never met Marg though.

Time to catch a wave, Badge.

I'm a big fan of water sports. Keeping a firm grip on your pole is crucial.

Save a horse, ride a cowboy. Long live John Wayne!

On Crab Claw Island doing the Top End by chopper as a Tourism Australia ambassador. Sweet gig.

Probably not the best place to practise my two-legged poodle walk.

Australia. We believe in a good time, a fair go ... and a dirty mo.

Stonehenge at Esperance. 2500 tonnes of granite – about as heavy as the All Blacks pack.

At Crocosaurus Cove in the Northern Territory for Tourism Australia. Do crocs eat ya whole? Nah, they spit that bit out.

Last time I was this far underground, I was almost 10 years old and dug a hole so deep in the backyard we almost hit China.

A Wallaby and a kangaroo. Meet Grace – snug as a bug in a rug!

Yarning with the locals on my bike trip across Australia with National Geographic.

Life's a long road. Hit it at pace.

Disconnect to reconnect.

Take the best and
wash off the rest!

Sinking my teeth into cage diving with great white sharks.

Getting a bit of D on the chassis.

Herding wild cattle bulls in the Northern Territory. I've still got scars to prove it.

On ya bike and into
the yonder. Take time
to find your freedom.

Do you reckon the llama copped a whiff?

Feeding a few Noahs
at sunset on the reef.

Nothing beats getting high in nature!

BADGERSAURUS

Underwear. AKA...

Boasters	Dick dacks
Toolies	Prong pointers
Scungies	Dick stickers
Lolly bags	Meat hangers
Budgie smugglers	Fish frighteners
Cluster busters	Slug huggers
CJs (cock jocks)	Snag hammocks
Cod wallopers	Tight white ball huggers

BADGERSAURUS

UKULELE

I picked up the guitar when I busted me leg a while back. When you get an injury it's pretty easy to just lay out on the couch playing video games or watching TV. And in my younger days that would have been the way to go. But I've come to understand that time is our most valuable commodity – and we should use it; to come out of something with a skill, with some knowledge, with something else.

I committed to learning on my mate's guitar and got a few songs down. Then I ended up buying a travel guitar and a ukulele. And the uke's just got its own vibe. It has this happy energy to it – this *really* happy energy – and the instant people hear it, they smile.

I like it because it's in line with my vibrations, with my values and my want to make people happy. Yeah, if you hadn't quite grabbed onto that top branch of what I'm about – it's that. Through all that I do – through humour and stories and rugby and whatever else I have, I'm about boosting up the goodness. And I've found the ukulele is the right instrument for that.

It's why I take my ukulele on my various journeys across the globe and around this great country. I sometimes find myself sitting in an airport when there's a delay – people are instantly blowing up, getting angry at something they can't control. And I'll just whip it out – the uke that is. And with one strum, you see and feel the energy change. They go from being in this negative state to being over-powered by a positive vibe. People smile, kids crowd around and dance. People get swept up in this instrument and that's pretty damn cool.

SHORTCUMMINS

Fart catcher
(faht-kachuh)

Bed, place of rest or relaxation, a naked flame near the point of flatulence, cupcake

Common usage: *Testing out a few fart catchers for the new high-rise shoebox.*

SHORTCUMMINS

THE BADGER v THE BACHELOR

Who'd have thought it? The Badger sharing his spirit and showing off the chassis on a loved-up reality TV show in front of millions.

I copped a bit, that's for sure. I guess the question I heard more than any other was, 'Why?' I was feeling pretty good about my life and my adventures. Next, I'm the star of a show I'd never watched before.

See, I can't be a bloke who blows a pretty large bugle about getting out there and experiencing things, seizing the moment and learning from pushing yourself into tight corners, and then shy away from an experience like *The Bachelor*.

So that's how The Badger ended up in a mansion packed with sheilas and cameras and guys answering to names like 'gaffer', 'best boy' and 'grip' and all sorts of other titles that could easily be taken out of context if you walked into a bar and introduced yourself as such.

For me, doing *The Bachelor* was about living up to a promise I made long ago – to be a bloke who pushes over the edge to see what happens. Regret is the only real fear I have in this life. I never want to look back and go, 'Hang on. I should've done this.' I don't want to die wondering or with the music in me. I want to always push forward. And if I make an arse out of myself? Then awesome. People can put shit on me for it for a while, but then they'll get it. At the same time, in my heart I'll say, 'You know what? I had a crack, I tried my best and, that way, I'm one step closer to reaching fulfillment in life.'

I believe that the people around you reflect what you're about. If you stuff around worrying about what others think, you're putting out a false vibe, and you'll end up attracting false people.

The other thing is that, with a show like *The Bachelor*, you're not just putting yourself out there by being on TV; you're hanging your emotions on the old Hills Hoist as well. And I want to be someone who shows blokes that there's nothing wrong with that.

As Aussie men, we're not good at putting our emotions out, and it leads to no good. So in taking on *The Bachelor*,

I'm hoping blokes understand that there's nothing wrong with talking about what's within. The days of hiding behind the wall of silence because, as an Australian male, showing feelings is 'not a done thing' or weak is officially bullshit.

To be The Bachelor takes courage. To do what I did in a public forum takes a supersized pair of balls. But this show was an opportunity for me to step outside my comfort zone and hopefully have a positive influence on some of the young Australians out there. To up our games a bit, as Aussie men.

To be honest, I struggled at the start. I was headbutting the system and the process.

Early on, I even put up a face that wasn't mine.

The first week especially, I was, 'Oh geez, look at all these cameras.' The 'face' went up straightaway. It was still me, but the face I was wearing had some of my edges smoothed out. But then I said to myself, 'C'mon mate, you're here to have a crack,' and I settled into it. Then, halfway through, I was feeling ok about things. I got on with it and I found some enjoyment in doing it because I was learning.

I go back to the blokes sitting on those couches watching it with their missus – 'cause they can argue all they want, but they know who they are – and I hope they see me showing emotions, and realise that if I can stand up and say that in front of cameras, even shed a tear, then they can do the same in their lives.

I'm not saying that I'm some guru sensitivity wizard that can make them do that, but I am someone who can bring people together to work at being their best. To be the best you that you can be. That's what I can inspire people to do.

As for my own learnings? After seeing how this crazy TV world all comes together and how it presents as it wants, maybe it's about me taking what I learnt about TV to go on a mission to try to start a different way of telling stories, one that involves the truth – a show about real stuff, about good news. So even after being basted and roasted, my understanding of that world is deeper and better than if I had sat on the sidelines and not got involved.

I don't have any regrets. I've hopefully come to raise the vibrations of the earth a bit, especially for blokes out there, and if I've done that, I'm happy.

WOMEN – AND NOT WANTING SOMETHING

Being locked away in a house full of women on *The Bachelor* meant learning more about womankind. I reflected deeply on how I've interacted with women in the past and I made some promises to myself about how I want to go about things better in the future.

There was a lot going on in that house. Each woman definitely had her own vibe happening. Some of these girls never really gave up their real selves, I reckon, keeping a mask on the whole time. Others chose not to, and I came to see how powerful that honesty and bravery was. Some girls struggled;

they had anxieties, a lack of confidence and emotional hang-ups. Ultimately what I really walked away with was how to talk to a girl without wanting anything from them.

For centuries, men have been raised to hunt. We go out on a mission, on a goal-orientated destination. That's how I thought it was with women, too, but it's not. Women are so much more than that. Certainly they don't have to be that target. They can be a friend, another perspective. Because of the way I saw women in the past, all of those learnings were hidden. Not any longer.

Every one of us has the masculine and the feminine. Every individual is both. And if you're only learning from half, then you're not really learning much.

I learnt to unlock a bit of the feminine on *The Bachelor*, and I can now sit down and have a yarn with a woman and not be thinking about where it's gonna lead and why I'm putting my time into this and whether it's 'worthwhile'.

Right from the beginning, I said to all the women, regardless of how things end up, I'd be their friend, their companion. We went on the ride together and I want the best for them because I genuinely care for them.

Yeah, The Badger found his feminine side in that house and there's nothing wrong with that.

SHORTCUMMINS

A good sort
(uh-good-sawt)

An attractive person, stunner, marriage material, keeper, a good bet, easy on the eye

Common usage: *Well, hello . . . aren't you a good sort!*

SHORTCUMMINS

A FEW CLUES
ABOUT CHIVALRY

When you want to make your woman feel special, here's a couple of courtesy clues.

➤ Offer to give up your seat on public transport. Birds will appreciate the courtesy even if they don't take you up on it.

➤ If someone takes offence at your offer, just smile. Most ladies would be rapt at your display of courtesy.

➤ Women don't usually wear bulky coats when they go out, as they wish to display their feminine attributes.

God love 'em! Still, always check for signs of cold. If you see your beloved exhibiting frostbite or random igloo-building, give her your jacket or coat or beanie immediately. (One of my brothers, who shall remain nameless [Nathan], was on the reverse side of this equation. Late one cold night, after a few beers and screaming for a feed, he jogged nude through a Maccas drive-thru while pushing a car tyre. They didn't give him a feed but the cashier threw a yellow rain coat at him. He whacked it on immediately, as his manhood began playing hide and seek. Chivalry goes both ways. She was a compassionate human being.)

➤ After a wild night doing the horizontal barn dance, don't pretend you're asleep. If she has to go home in the morning, put your pluggers on and walk her to the cab. It's only a little thing but word gets around and if you're single you may find yourself being sought after by more Cirque du Soleil performers.

➤ Communicate and compliment. After a wild night of rodeo riding, give her a bell or a text (no anatomy pics). Don't mention her flexibility, but compliment her on her personality. Or both. Both is also good.

SHORTCUMMINS

Like a tree full of galahs
(luyk-uh-tree-fool-ov-guh'lahs)

To be rowdy, to display bad manners, sheilas' catch up

Common usage: *Those kids are like a tree full of galahs.*

SHORTCUMMINS

HOW TO FINISH UP WITH A BIRD

The beginning of a relationship is usually pretty full-on. Blokes and sheilas turn into a couple of oversexed octopi, and life is grand.

After a while, things mellow a bit and both parties begin to see little faults with the other.

Usually the female regains her sense of smell and will offer the bloke, who is generally oblivious to most things, some self-improvement hints. He can't understand how, if he was perfect four weeks ago, he can all of a sudden be in need of serious emotional and physical panel-beating.

Sometimes it works out, sometimes it doesn't.

If a bloke feels the relationship has run its course, he must be very careful in making his next move.

The first thing to do is to discuss the situation with your other half. If there is no joy to be found, then you must cut each other loose.

If she feels the same way you do, then it's easy.

If you broach the subject and she looks at you like you've just killed the invisible swordsman, you're in strife!

Don't tell her by text as this is poor form. She will show her mates and they will confirm you really are a giant bastard.

Don't tell her by phone because that is the move of a weak bastard, not wanting to deal with emotion. Don't tell her while in public. If she freaks out, you have nowhere to run and you will look like a swine. Every bugger within earshot will enjoy the proceedings, thanking God it's not them. Including me.

Try to be alone with her in a quiet place.

Show compassion and understanding but stick to your guns, 'cause there's no use flogging a dead horse. Accept that you're different people and no one is to blame. Expect tears, from her as well, and then make a cautious retreat.

Down the track, your paths may cross, so do not speak poorly of her to anyone, even if she does of you.

Hopefully you can have a civil conversation in the future,

and you can get along as friends. If not, lock your doors at night and beef up security.

It's a jungle out there.

BADGERSAURUS

Nervous as a . . .

long-tailed cat in a room full of
rocking chairs

bag of cats at a greyhound meet

gypsy with a mortgage

mother kangaroo in a room full
of pickpockets

BADGERSAURUS

LAND DOWN UNDER

My old man runs a landscaping business and his crew often features some colourful characters.

On one gig he was talking to the client, a bossy sheila with a backyard like Suncorp Stadium.

This old duck knew what she wanted.

'Up the side, I want kangaroo paws either side of the path,' she said.

Dad nodded, and then yelled to a couple of his crew who'd started work, 'GREEN SIDE UP!'

The sheila went on. 'Out front I want a mix of native flowers and frangipanis.'

Dad nodded again. Then rolled his eyes and yelled to the crew, 'GREEN SIDE UP!'

'Along the patio I want ferns to shade the house from the northern sun.'

Dad didn't hear. He was red in the face and screaming, 'GREEN SIDE UP!'

Finally, the sheila blew her stack.

'Mr Cummins, I'm giving very detailed instructions for my garden landscaping and you keep yelling, "GREEN SIDE UP!" What the hell are you talking about?'

'Sorry ma'am,' says Dad. 'I've got a couple of Kiwis laying turf out there.'

THE UNFORGIVEN

As much as I love to get out there and do my own thing, there are times when you have to toe the line.

When I was a young rooster, our family would whack on our good clobber, pile into the Mitsubishi Star wagon and march off to Sunday mass. My sisters were always pretty well-behaved, so they had a fair chance of going to heaven. My brothers and I were a whole different story. I was pretty sure heaven didn't want us but I was also positive that hell couldn't handle us.

The whole church thing was a struggle for the Cummins clan. For a mob with the attention span of a goldfish to have to rattle off prayers for one hour, it was tough – on the parents especially.

For me, the best way to endure the hour of power was to whisper something to one of my brothers or sisters in an attempt to make them laugh or get filthy at me. Hopefully this would attract the attention of Mum or Dad and the culprit would be in line for a serve later on.

The ultimate plan was to smash out an SBD (Silent But Deadly) so those around you would start gagging during the main parts of the service.

I was gifted in that department and had no problems making the whole congregation believe there was a dangerous gas leak and doom was imminent. The look on the faces of elderly God-fearing victims with their eyes rolled back and hankies over their mouths, sensing this was their last moment on earth, caused me no end of joy.

One particular Sunday, my younger brother tried to reach the dizzy heights that I had achieved the previous Sunday. He whispered he was about to cut loose just as the priest was discussing the Ten Commandments.

Well, he must have broken the eleventh one exactly at that moment. 'Thou shalt not shit yourself.' The poor bastard followed through with the power of a jet engine. I lost it. Dad stared at me, I pointed to the offending arse, and the old bird with the walking frame standing behind us slumped into her seat.

What a top morning!

On the way home, my brother sat in a hovercraft-like pose, not wanting to make the carnage any worse. God, it was a great day.

I recall another Sunday, we were running late. The fact it was a beautiful sunny day meant the Cummins boys were contemplating atheism again.

The old man was a stickler for being on time and was threatening us with various forms of medieval torture if we didn't move it.

Dad started the van and I dived in as he slammed the door, almost making me an amputee. As we roared down the long driveway, like the Batmobile launching out of the Batcave, Dad was already giving us a burst. Once he got a head of steam up, he'd go off track and blame us for everything including starting World War II.

As we sped along the road, two wood ducks marched out and made the mistake of not looking right or left.

Dad had turned his head to give us a final spray when life ended quickly for those poor beaked bastards. One found a home in the nudge bar while the other started a career as a third windscreen wiper. Dad, fearless campaigner that he is, didn't miss a beat and roared on to our heavenly destination. As the kids ambled into the soul-saving session, I helped the old fella remove our unwilling hitchhikers. As we walked in to acknowledge our sins, I asked the old man if the ducks would go to heaven. He informed me that they were in hell, exactly where I'd be if I was ever late again! But he did have a grin on his face.

I'm sure there's a lesson there, somewhere.

The Honey Badger Guide to Life # 12

Listen – we've got two ears and one mouth. Work out the ratio for talking and listening.

One cock in the fowl house

(wun-kok-in-dhuh-fowl-hows)

One person in charge, one rooster in the chook pen, chain of command

Common usage: *You can't come in mate, there's only one cock in this fowl house.*

ROGUE CHAMPIONS

Kurt Fearnley AO

23 March 1981

If you want the definition of a champion, take a gander at this bloke.

His list of achievements is as long as the old man's TAB losing sequence. He just doesn't give up.

As a young cat, he was up against it. Born with sacral agenesis, a devastating illness, he seemed destined to a limited existence in the confines of a wheelchair. Kurt had other plans! Despite his initial lifespan diagnosis being one week, he decided to give that the bird and instead became one of Australia's greatest athletes.

© Dean Lewins/AAP

No doubt positive reinforcement from family and friends helped him along the road to success, but it doesn't matter what anyone says – in the end, it's up to you.

- Thirteen Paralympic Games medals, including three gold

- Five World Championship medals, including four gold

- Four Commonwealth Games medals, including two gold

While he was conquering the sporting world, he also attained a degree in human movement and began a teaching career.

You reckon that's enough? No way, Jose. This winner grabbed life by the nuts and wanted more.

Despite all he has done, his greatest achievement has been his marriage to his beautiful wife, Sheridan, and his pigeon pair, Harry and Emilia. What great role models those kids have.

In 2009, he took on the Kokoda Track. This bloke dragged his arse 96 kms over mountain ranges, rivers, swamps and various other shitfights to raise awareness for Beyond Blue and Movember.

He deflected all accolades for his efforts, instead heaping praise on the young Aussie troops who gave everything in 1942. Kurt spoke glowingly of young blokes like Corporal John Metson who, after enduring all manner of disease and depravation, was shot in both legs. He refused a stretcher, so others could be saved, and dragged himself along the track for three weeks, until he was shot and killed.

My brother Luke has walked the track and my sister Bernadette has climbed Mt Kinabalu in Malaysia. They claimed the mozzies had pilots and the blowflies had saddles. It's a tough gig, even for someone with legs. I'll find out soon.

Kurt Fearnley is used to doing it tough – he's made an art of it. To win four New York marathons, you have to have some ticker and attitude.

Before attempting the track, he said, 'It's going to be tough, it's going to be hard but it's doable.'

The hardest thing for this former Young Australian of the Year would have been dragging that massive set of clackers he possesses across that mountain range.

Only a man with nuts of iron could match his achievements. This bloke should be wearing a cape and staying well clear of kryptonite. And while his list of achievements is endless, the joy on his face while carrying the Aussie flag at the 2018 Commonwealth Games was the icing on the cake.

Take a bow, Kurt Fearnley. You're the man.

WELSHIES
SAVE THE DAY

There are some old country towns in Australia where rugby hasn't lost an inch of character. One such place comes to mind: deep in the outback, where outhouses are commonplace, to wear jeans with pluggers is considered formal wear and a good old handshake and a carton of beer can solve the worst of disputes between neighbours.

These joints are still out there and they're worth seeing.

I was visiting my brother Luke in one such place, when he got a call from his mate Adso.

'Hey, Cummo, we're short of troops, can you belt down and give us a hand . . .? And bring some more cattle with ya!'

I quickly realised the rugby team was short of players and found myself wanting to be part of the crusade. Luke replied, 'Roger that, how many do we need, Adso?'

'We got seven, we need twelve to avoid a forfeit, so ... five, I reckon. There's a backpackers' hostel up the road, I hear there are some Welshies [aka Welsh rugby players] in there. Grab them!'

In we went and after interrupting a couple in the nest, we found the right dorm.

'Hey, are you buggers Welsh . . .?'

'Yeah, why?'

'Get ya boots, I'll explain on the way!'

Just like that the cavalry was charging into battle, with three Welsh fruit pickers covered in red dirt and smelling like bum sweat, in a less than trustworthy four-wheel steed.

The Honey Badger Guide to Life # 13

Learn to lose - do you want to be right or happy? Sometimes it's best to just let things go. Stand for something, not everything.

We turn up just before kick-off to see our group of lads not even dressed and one or two of them suckin' on lung busters. The other team had a full squad of 22 and were running drills on the field in a neatly regimented manner. The ref marched up to our captain and said, 'You must take the field now or you will forfeit!'

Barefoot and with balls of steel, he asked the ref to flip the coin. Our mob won the toss and elected to kick off, so the other team had to wait. This gave our troops time to finish their darts and gear up. So with twelve men in a fifteen-man game we took the field. Somehow, in all the disorganised chaos – the Welshies playing the game of their lives, still wondering how they were dragged into it – we got the job done. We bloody won the bastard! 22–15.

SHORTCUMMINS

A million-dollar airport with a ten-cent control tower

(uh-milyuhn-doluh-airpawt-widh-uh-ten-sent-kuhn'trohl-towuh)

Great physique with minimal neurological capacity, great assets but shot upstairs, potentially a great idea, an ashtray on a motorbike

Common usage: *Ivan Drago out of Rocky IV is a million-dollar airport with a ten-cent control tower.*

SHORTCUMMINS

BADGERSAURUS

Why fight when you can . . .

Blue

Biff

Barney

Stoush

Donnybrook

Stacks on

Ding dong

Go the knuckle

Go off like a bucket of prawns in the sun

BADGERSAURUS

FEMINISM

Righto, I've said the F word.

If you've ever longed for a boot in the twins, or wanted a bird to hand you a big cup of shut the hell up, voice a stupid opinion on this topic.

The very idea of a feminist strikes fear into the hearts of old school mortal men. Some blokes have strange visions of big sheilas with hairy armpits, US-marine haircuts and covered head to toe with tough stickers.

There is so much more to feminism than that.

Fact is, sheilas have had a tough run through history. Blokes would chase 'em, marry 'em, and then take 'em for granted. An old fella said to me once at a shindig, 'Mate, I married her, I don't have to dance anymore.'

That may be so, but run with that plan at your peril.

Around the turn of the twentieth century, birds all over the world were starting to get jack of being treated as second-class citizens. The suffrage movement was born. Women protested in the streets, demanding the right to vote.

My personal take on feminism is pretty straightforward. Men and women are equal, but not the same. We all bring something different to the table.

There are champions and cockheads in every race, breed, colour or gender. I've known some wonderful women and I've met some wild critters.

Some of the more extreme variety would gladly hack off your tackle with a meat cleaver and then claim that blokes are the root of all evil. But the only true evil I've perpetrated on this planet was left in a Delhi dunny after the 2010 Commonwealth Games.

The Honey Badger Guide to Life # 14

Don't criticise – let people find their way. Give them a leg-up, not a drag down.

In all seriousness, many women are captains of industry and command respect for their intellect and achievements. They've got a fair bit to deal with, even from other women, who can be far tougher than blokes could ever be.

In my 30 years on the earth, I found the way to get the best out of a bird is to treat her with respect. We all deserve to be treated that way. Put simply, treat her as you would your mum or your sister.

Birds deserve a bit more than, 'How ya going, luv?'

Talk is cheap, actions are the best chance to show your woman you care for her.

As the old bloke says, you catch more flies with honey.

THE 'OLD BULL'

Everyone has an old man story, whether it be dad jokes, a fishing tale or doing something strange that only dads can do. But not everyone has a dad like mine...

We were heading home from a fishing tour of Rainbow Beach when we saw a bloke observing what looked to be a snake on the side of the road. So Dad pulled up to see if he could help.

Dad: 'G'day mate, what have we got here?'

Bloke: 'Looks like a tiger!'

Dad: 'Nah, it's definitely a snake!'

We wandered back to the car and, as we drove off, the bloke was still staring at us with a look that suggested medication was required.

Another time, when the old man and his mates hired a houseboat for the weekend, all seemed to be going swimmingly until they opted for more of a liquid diet. They decided to pull up on a sand island and play some footy in the sun. As the afternoon wore on and the tide went out, you could hear a slight cracking sound, but no one took much notice and the game continued. As the sun began to set, they piled back into the boat to find a rock on the floor of the deck. A few beers later, they realised the rock had punctured through from underneath the vessel. They'd parked on a rock. So the old man called the owner to explain:

Dad: 'Hey, mate, how are you going?'

Owner: 'Good, thanks, is everything ok?'

Dad: 'Yeah, we have a slight ding in the boat!'

Owner: 'Don't worry, we'll look at it when you get back.'

Dad: 'Well, mate, it's a bit more than a ding, it's more like a puncture!'

Owner: 'A puncture, bloody hell, how did this happen? Never mind, there's a patch kit on board.'

Dad: 'Well, mate, its more of a hole, the patch kit won't work.'

Owner: 'WTF have you done to the boat? How big is the hole?'

Dad: 'Oh, I'd say a metre by a metre . . .'

He sunk the bastard.

★ ★ ★

The 'Old Bull'

My old man has final-stage prostate cancer. To date, he has defied the odds, the doctors and the statistics and is still charging around the place. He is currently in Hawaii on a surfing trip. And has recently endured his 75th bout of radium treatment (cook-off, as he calls it). Doctors don't know of anyone that has been able to withstand that amount of radiation. Dad said his turds now glow in the dark and he saves heaps on electricity.

One day he turned up at the clinic and there was a waiting room full of very sad men, the mood was quite sombre. In front of all the patients, to make Dad feel comfortable, the nurse lady asked, 'Good morning, is there anything we can do to improve your experience?'

Dad: 'Yes, can we change the music that's played while you throw us in the oven?'

Lady: 'Sure, is it "Rainforest" tunes or "Waterfall" noises you would like to change?'

Dad: 'Both!'

Lady: 'Ok, what would you like us to change it to?'

Dad: 'Meatloaf nice and loud, 'cause we are all gunna burn in there!'

This is the kind of bloke he is. He takes things head on and makes the most difficult of situations as entertaining as possible. It's a good way to be.

THE OLD
WATERING HOLE

Old rugby players never die . . . they just smell that way.

These five former leatherheads I know had played lower-grade country footy together since they were young critters. They all retired from the footy field in their thirties but vowed to keep in touch.

One of them had the great idea to celebrate their 40th birthdays in style with a reunion lunch.

'Great idea,' the other blokes agreed. 'Let's go to The Marlin – the barmaid's wear short skirts and it's open until 3 am.' Each had a skinful of neck oil, and a top arvo and evening was had by all.

For their 50th birthdays the boys teamed up again. 'Let's go to The Marlin – the bistro is great and they've got a fantastic craft beer selection.' They laughed like drains, reminisced about old times and were all in taxis by midnight.

Ten years later, the same golden oldies reunited to toast their 60th year on the planet. A quick consensus was reached on the venue. 'Let's go to The Marlin – they've got a wine cellar and an undercover carpark.' The sunshine boys had a solid gargle and were home in time for dinner.

When it came time to reunite and celebrate their 70th birthdays, the old boys were of one voice yet again. 'Let's go to The Marlin. They've got wheelchair access and a pensioner lunch special.'

But when the boys reunited to celebrate their 80th birthdays the natives were restless. 'Let's try somewhere new,' they agreed. 'What about The Marlin? We've never been there before.'

THE BADGER KICKS A FEW GOALS WITH AERIAL PING PONG

I've met a lot of people on my travels. People brimming with life experience and those starting out on their journeys of discovery. I've met many good blokes – even those who persist in the cultivation of feral hair possums (dreadlocks) – and some truly wonderful women. I've met the eccentric, the intelligent, the brave and the bold, the toothless and the ruthless. I've also spent time with the selfish, the simple and the spectacularly annoying.

I've also found myself in the middle of nowhere dancing about with a sport that's always intrigued but which I've never really engaged with before: Australian Rules Football.

It was on my travels across the bottom of the country, belting between SA and WA, that I came to feel this curious yellow lump of leather on my foot. I was invited to hit up a training run with some confident young blokes who like to get about their footy on the weekend dressed in singlets and short shorts.

Obviously AFL's not my sport – but that doesn't matter, because as Australians we generally take to whatever footy we can get. And so it was, nearly 800 clicks west of Adelaide on a sandy, remote oval overlooking the Great Australian Bite that The Badger had a run at Aussie Rules with a bunch of local players.

Now I may or may not have kicked a few goals on my non-preferred foot from 40 metres out on a tight angle – but it was more than a few solid scoring shots that left an impression on me from this experience.

The captain of the local team called me into this curious 'contact drill' that was basically a game of chicken between him and me.

'I'm gonna run at you full pelt and you're gonna run at me,' he barked as an explanation. It set my mind spinning given I know these AFL blokes aren't exactly big on the contact side of things.

Righto. So off he goes, with the speed of a wounded gazelle, and runs straight at me. I do the same and, at the right moment, throw a shoulder and drop him.

This moment stands out 'cause he just bounced back up and we had a good laugh about it. He knew I'd put him on his arse but he wanted to test himself – to have a crack. We've all been on our arses but it's getting up that counts. And that's what these country blokes are about – they breed 'em tough so they're willing to put their hand up, dive in and actually push themselves.

I look at that spirit and I immediately think of our ANZAC forefathers – they were the same way. They were the best bloody stockmen, the best sportsmen, true gentlemen and characters full of class. They stood for what they believed in and they never shirked – they put their heads down and ran straight, regardless of what was coming for them in the other direction and what the outcome would probably be.

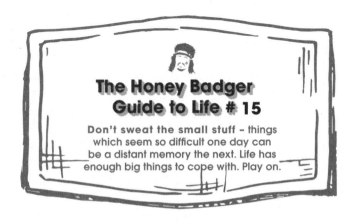

The Honey Badger Guide to Life # 15

Don't sweat the small stuff – things which seem so difficult one day can be a distant memory the next. Life has enough big things to cope with. Play on.

Young blokes get a rough ride these days, and even though I reckon Millennials have lost a bit of fight, with everyone getting so bloody offended about this and that, what I saw with these footy blokes who are stuck out in the in the bowels of SA made me realise we've still got it. They don't care about finding fault or outrage, about whinging over petty shit. They're for getting out there and having a crack, and as I see it, these next generation fellas are carrying on some of the hardened traits of our forefathers.

The other thing I thought about, as I waved goodbye and headed back out to the flat and long bitumen connecting this sparse patch of the country, was about the importance of footy, or group activities like footy, in places where by city standards there isn't a lot to do.

A footy club out in Woop Woop is more than just a 'footy club' – it's a beating heart and so bloody important. It brings together these blokes and their families, it forms bonds between them, it gives them something to look forward to each and every week and just belts a sense of camaraderie and brotherhood into the place.

This is really important – especially in rural areas, where, unfortunately, mental health and the suicide rate can be a big issue. Out here, having a sporting team is like medicine, because it brings everyone together to heal and bond. You've instantly got a group of mates and a support base that you can rely on through thick and thin.

In a small town, footy of any code pulls people together instead of keeping them separated and isolated. The club functions and social events bring the whole joint into concert and really drive a loving, friendly community.

And I reckon we could all learn something from this sense of belonging – especially those of us stuck in city towers not knowing who even lives next door.

Life is about getting involved and having a crack – holding out a hand and saying hello. Only when we do this will we have the communities we once did – full of people we can rely on and ask for help.

And who we can help in turn.

BADGERSAURUS

So ugly they've got a . . .

Head like a half-eaten pie

Face like a smashed crab

Smile like a burst sausage

Head like a half-sucked mango

Mouth like a cat's bum

Face like a yard of tripe

Face like a bulldog chewing on
a wasp

Face like a kicked-in cake tin

Smile like a fox chewing on guts

Head like a beaten favourite

Face like the northbound end
of a southbound cow

Body like a busted sofa

Dial like a wombat licking piss
off a nettle

Hair like a bush pig's arse

BADGERSAURUS

THICK SKIN

What are we offended about today?

As a society, we've changed and sometimes for the better. Nowadays, we don't believe the half-truths we're told by our political masters, banks and other institutions. We question most things and that's a plus.

On the flip side, many people are pretty damn precious and desperately seek something to be filthy about. All rights, no responsibility.

Australia was once a laidback nation – it's how I remember growing up. People said their piece, had the odd argument and then got on with it. No one's opinion was worth more than anyone else's, whether you ate steak or lettuce.

A couple of years ago, I was on a bus coming back from white-water rafting near Cairns. The tour guide gave us the lunch option of 'roadkill or dolphin'. Funny bastard. A few people on the bus were horrified – I was stoked. He got it.

We all need to stop being overly sensitive.

Many years ago, Dad was playing footy for the Mullumbimby Moonshiners and after the game, both teams rocked up to the club house to sink a couple. About 5.30 pm, they drew the hot chook raffle and, as luck would have it, Dad had the winning ticket. I had a hunger that could restart the Cold War and was dribbling with delight as the lukewarm dead bird was being passed overhead to us.

To my horror, people began sampling and groping the unlucky chook as it made its final journey. By the time the chook arrived in my hands, it was a greasy skeleton with a flap of skin across its arse. I was filthy. Dad's response, 'Give that skinny bastard a feed and buy another ticket.'

No need to get upset, just play on!

Our opinions on many things may differ, but we all deserve to be heard. Just because someone is louder than you doesn't mean they're right.

Your opinion is just that – yours – and, like arseholes, we've all got 'em. Mind you there is a certain responsibility attached to what you say, so think about it.

If I'm dirty with someone, I'll tell 'em, no beating around the bush. It's easy that way. If I think a bird is a great sort, I'll tell her. If they go to all the trouble of putting on the war paint and committing to some minor panel-beating, they deserve a compliment.

Recently, I was talking to my neighbour as we watched a crow ripping into the rubbish bin. I stated that the crow was so black, it probably farted soot. He looked at me like I just punched out a nun!

We need to get the hell on with each other and allow everyone the space to talk openly and freely.

As Aussies, we've got it pretty good. The sun's going to rise tomorrow and, if you're in Queensland, probably the next few weeks after that.

Tomorrow, you'll slip into some double pluggers and do your thing.

We've got footy on the weekends, a lick from rover and attitude from the cat.

Embrace the real things life offers, and don't find fault in every uttered word.

Full steam ahead!

Up the guts and into 'em

(up-dhuh-guts-uhn-intooh-uhm)

Go direct, bite the bullet, charge forward, take no prisoners, have a crack or a dig, take 'em on

Common usage: *I'm gonna march into the boardroom, up the guts and into 'em.*

THE CATS IN THE CRADLE

'I love cats, but I couldn't eat a whole one!'

I've heard that story a few times, but I personally admire the buggers. How many animals are there that get nine shots at life? Bloody extraordinary.

My experience with cats has been brief but intense. It all started when the doorbell rang, I opened the door and looked down to see a small cat standing there. My first thought was, 'What a gifted cat! I mean, it's either a lot taller than it looks or it's got a wicked reach.' I asked Dad if we could keep the bugger. I was eleven and very responsible.

The old man looked at it and said we can keep it, until we find its rightful owners, on these conditions:

1. It must stay outside.

2. You will look after it.

3. If it bogs inside the house, I'll use your pillow case to dispose of the evidence.

Just like that, Stretch became a member of the family. We consulted Whitey, a feline expert (a friend of the family who once had a cat), to see if it was a boy or a girl. Walking back from the observation room (the shed), Whitey, with a look of conviction, asserted that it was a male. As in, it had the twig and berries, rod and tackle, meat and potatoes, the bat and balls . . . you know the drill.

'At least we don't have to get the thing de-sexed,' proclaimed the old man. Things were going great, we finally had a family pet for us all to play with. As the weeks rolled by, we noticed that Stretch was getting involved in a lot of what only could be described as late-night fighting. Then we soon noticed that Stretch was getting bigger and bigger. It seemed a little strange at first, as we weren't feeding him any more than usual. Soon, it just got weird. I thought he had swallowed one of Dad's work boots, his guts were that massive.

One day, Stretch just seemed to vanish. We couldn't find him anywhere, until we heard some strange noises coming from behind the shed. As we went over to suss it out, we couldn't believe our eyes. Our male cat had just popped out six kittens. It must have been a bloody first for our neck of the woods. I mean, what are the chances? He'd defied biology. No one was more shocked than Whitey.

I think the old man was really excited like the rest of us, but he did really well not to show it. You know when you are so happy that you don't blink for a while, and ya face goes blank? He must have been in a complete state of gratitude. Everyone started to choose their own cat. There was Tabby, Speed (the slowest), Cheetah, the Russian, Stevens (because he made some good noises) and Bogger. We put all of them through their paces, trained them hard and got them ready for the big bad world.

Like many of the pets that followed in the footsteps of our pregnant male cat Stretch, it was always an adventure and a journey for us all. Stretch paved the way for two future guinea pigs that we rescued from a science lab at school, both dog-food addicts. These guinea pigs were ripped. It's rare to see bulging biceps on creatures of that nature. If they could talk, I'm sure the first thing they would have asked for would have been a set of dumbbells, a bench press and a skull-and-bones tattoo. They were tough buggers.

The old man always seemed to support the pets he inherited. In a strange twist of fate, he ended up with a goat called Bluey. He always had a thing for goats. I'm glad he was able to bond with Bluey, they understood each other. I think it's because Bluey was the only one that never got tired of listening to the old man's ramblings.

ROADKILL & LIPS

I recently found myself on a walkabout in some of
Australia's more remote stretches of outback.

Ok, it wasn't a true walkabout in the sense of how this
country's first inhabitants do things – and without pluggers
no less! But it was an excursion to get my feet in the sand all
the same – even if I was just driving between depots.

You'll have probably realised by now that I love going
rogue in the bush. As much as I love getting out there for
the seclusion and the space and the very real power it settles
in me, I also love getting out there to meet the characters.
Because to live remotely is to do things differently – and,
yeah, I'm a bloke who does things differently. And *The*

Honey Badger Guide to Life is a great way to explain my life. Sheep are stupid animals and to conform and walk the same muddy path as a daggy beast makes no sense to me.

On this recent meander I found myself belting about the bottom of South Australia for National Geographic on a run that'd eventually spit me and the trusty out in Western Australia. I met a few rogue characters along the track. And I even did some graft with a few of them – to understand what they're about and what a day in their life looks like. To be a bloke open to understanding others, I figure you've got to peel back the sunnies and squint into the blinding reality of someone else's world.

That was how I met Lips. Now Lips works for one of the more remote councils in SA – near the town of Ceduna, a fishing joint named for a local Aboriginal word that means to sit and rest. And you could do that there – sit and rest – but not Lips, who, as part of his work, hits the highway to clean up the poor bloody animals turned to blood and bone by fast-moving road trains.

Lips likes to jab the tourists who come out here with a line about where they'll likely see their first kangaroo – it's not at the zoo or foraging in the outback – it's wheels up on the side of the road, dead as Julius Caesar.

It falls to blokes like Lips to make sure this roadkill – out this way most of 'em wombats – don't make for unexpected hairy speed bumps. While I reckon most of us think of wombats as these cute and cuddly little things, out here they're bred big and tough. Powerful buggers. In fact, their hind legs are so strong they've been known to use them to lure a fox or a dog or dingo towards its burrow. It'll go in head first, and it'll leave its bum showing because its bum's so tough that a dog can bite it with no result – it won't go through the fur. But the wombat will squat down a little bit, so there's a gap between the roof of the den and the wombat's arse, so when the dog or the fox puts its head in to try to bite, the wombat does a really fast power squat and crushes the attacker's skull on the roof of the burrow. Yeah, they're pretty powerful but have bugger-all road sense, so when they meet metal on a highway at speed, well, just hope one of your mates is a panel-beater.

Lips offered me a gig as an assistant wombat carcass removalist. He threw me a metal hook and I got to work. It's tough work. You tend to cop a whiff before you even get too close to a carcass, especially with the sun blazing down and a thousand maggots playing their role in ecology.

According to Lips, what you want to do is get the beast around the spine – because that holds it together. Trust me when I say you don't want to be having a few goes hooking a wombat corpse as you'll definitely throw up. Then you give it a decent Aussie burial away from the road, right? Not quite. You just fling it further into the scrub and the sand so it's not a menace to transport.

Lips and I drove up and down Ceduna doing this. This is his job five days a week – a job in the middle of nowhere, talking to no one, shifting rotting animal bits under an angry sun while being hugged by a putrid scent. For most of us that sounds like a tough day at the office. But for Lips this is the way it is and he wouldn't change it.

When not shifting flesh and fur, Lips and I chatted about what he takes from what seems like a hard, lonely, depressing job.

But, as Lips sees it, he's a man of wealth because he has found what he wants. He has freedom and time. He also has a great stillness around him, a peace. Lips likes the quiet. He doesn't want any stress and he can't imagine living in the city.

The Honey Badger Guide to Life # 16

Solitude – at times, you need to be on your pat (Malone). Ask hard questions. You can fool everyone else, but you can't fool yourself.

I enjoyed spending time with Lips – even if it meant inhaling the smell of death and wearing some dodgy hi-vis get-up in 120 degree heat.

Because Lips knows what he wants and he's found it, he has peace of mind. He has no regrets. And that's the best way to live life – to follow a feeling or a passion, to follow what it is that makes you happy.

My biggest fear in life is regret. The last thing I want to do is be on my deathbed thinking about that sort of shit and all the things I didn't embrace or experience or act on.

I salute you, Lips. You and your bloody smelly job.

One man's highway to hell is another man's stairway to heaven.

Back passage

(bak-pasij)

Anus, blurter, brown eye, quoit, ring, date, freckle, sun-dried tommie, muffler, tailpipe

Common usage: *Bali belly turned my back passage into a tap.*

SATELLITES

Did ya hear about the two satellites getting together?
Yeah, they got married, and the wedding wasn't much
but the reception was incredible.

The Honey Badger Guide to Life # 17

Affordability - live according to your means. Getting into too much debt will only cause you pain. There's so much to enjoy without spending a fortune.

Thunder box
(thunduh-boks)

Toilet, bogger, s-bend, pisser, rose bowl, the office

Common usage: *I'm going offline for a bit, gonna hit the thunder box.*

THE BADGER
IN A BOBSLED

I reckon every bloke who's ever watched the Winter Olympics has at some time thought, 'Yeah, I'd definitely give that a crack,' and I'm not just talking about the Russian ice dancers.

It's why a few years back I slipped into some Lycra and familiarised myself with what it feels like to hold another man, tightly, from behind. Because The Badger got a sniff of more than just a few sweaty blokes – I got a taste for bobsledding.

It happened via an epic and icy adventure that I had through Alberta. The opportunity to try bobsledding out was something I jumped at. And I immediately loved it. Why wouldn't ya – pulling four Gs and hitting close to 130 km/h in a coffin on skates. Being me, I wanted to give it a proper crack – and I wanted to see if I could make it into the Aussie team. And I was serious. I wanted a piece of this. I wanted to stand on a bloody Olympic podium one day.

That's why, when I came out of rugby, I didn't go and sign up to get a job. Instead, I put six months of my life into training for bobsled, for a new direction in life, a new set of experiences that might feed me.

I always felt rugby gave me a pretty good athletic make-up and that finely tuned chassis may one day lead me to transition to something else. Bobsled incorporates everything from sprinting, to power and endurance – mental toughness and discipline too – stuff that I understood and had gained from rugby.

I met Heath Spence, the Aussie bobsled pilot, then threw myself into the training. I worked for months. Bloody hard work. Because I wanted this more than a drunk fella with a late-night lamb-and-gravy sandwich.

Training consisted of a lot of short explosive sprints with sprint coaches, a lot of movement and flexibility, and more squats than an Instagram model.

Tough work but I really wanted this. I wanted to get in and get some results with the team. I felt I could bring some energy too, bring some noise to the sport and help chase a medal – because there was no reason why the Aussies shouldn't be up there and having a proper go.

So I went over and got into it with the guys. We went ballistic and did 25 runs in three days – chasing the Olympic requirements, which also included an event.

I'll be honest with you – it's all economy class in those sleds. You bounce around and hit your head and your body comes out bruised; the G forces push your head down into your arsehole and you just hold on and stare at the floor. And then it's over. The adrenalin and the power, the technique, the explosiveness, the athleticism and the teamwork – all those qualities and challenges made me want to be a part of it.

Of course, I ended up on *The Bachelor* and not the bobsled team. I was gutted to miss a shot at the Olympics. It came down to some ridiculous triviality apparently – the fact I hadn't completed a component in a specific time period, hadn't got the runs done in the right month or some stupid thing.

Yeah – I was stingin'. This wasn't just some try-out for me – I'd thrown myself fully into it. I'd trained so bloody hard, stacked on 6 kilos of muscle, and become 20 per cent quicker over 20 metres. I was pumped for the quest for Olympic gold.

And for it to all unravel because someone in a position of authority decided to pull the thread and claim I was ineligible – it hurt. I was bloody filthy, in fact.

But you have to get over it and move on. And it's not to say that I can't dust this one off and get back in the sled. That's right, folks, let's put it out there and state it for the record that's what I do want to do. I want back in the bobsled. I want back in the Lycra. I want to show people what I can do. I want to fly down a track at speeds that scare the shit out of me. I want to live – fast, dangerous and beautiful.

Watch this space, Lycra fans.

SHORTCUMMINS

Gone up and over and head over biscuit

(gon-up-uhn-ohvuh-uhn-hed-ohvuh-biskuht)

To fall over, lose balance, stack it, wipe-out, top heavy

Common usage: *I was as full as the last bus and I've gone up and over and head over biscuit.*

SHORTCUMMINS

SURF'S UP

Surfing's pretty calming for me. It's something I do a fair bit with my family at Christmas and I've also done it in South Africa and even in Japan – and hooley dooley if that wasn't colder than the soul on any one of those Kardashian chicks.

Sometimes when I go surfing I find myself just sitting and watching. I'm just scoping the waves and feeling the motion of the ocean.

And then someone will slide into a wave and pull past me and I can see what they're experiencing; the fun they're having, the fact they're at one with the ocean, and anything else that may have been bugging them has been pushed aside as they are here, in this moment, and cleansed. I see that and then think, 'Time to catch a wave, Badge.'

The Honey Badger
Guide to Life # 18

Smile – it's good for you and great
for the world. A little effort can light
it up for everyone.

All over it like an orphan on a T-bone steak

(awl-ohvuh-uht-luyk-uhn-awfuhn-on-uh-tee-bohn-stayk)

Territorial, killer instinct, committed, to have intent, hungry as

Common usage: *After six months at sea he was all over her like an orphan on a T-bone steak.*

ALL IN THE FAMILY

In my family there's sickness – I think most people know we're grappling with cancer and cystic fibrosis. There's definitely some rainy days coming soon.

But family is always the most important thing in my life. The Cummins mob are close, not geographically these days but spiritually and emotionally.

There's been times when we walk away from that, and as a young fella it's easier to not fully understand what you've got. With my clan, if you start to lose sight of what's important or make some selfish decisions, you'll get skull-dragged back in and sat down in the middle – 'Right, get back in here, sit down and shut up.' And we'll get back to taking the piss and have some fun and have a laugh until that feeling of family comes rushing back. Because without family, what have you really got?

It's why I went to play footy in Japan in 2014. I could have kept on with all the bullshit things – like notoriety, fame, status – or I could go over there and get stuck in and get stuff done and know there's some financial back-up for when the shit hits the fan. And it will.

The Honey Badger Guide to Life # 19

Acceptance – life's unfair. Accept that life will throw unreasonable challenges at you. It's how you deal with them that sets you apart.

Along the way, a few people said that it must have been a tough decision for me to make – to end one dream with the Wallabies and head overseas to chase some coin that would then help out with family. For me there's no comparison – on one side is a lot of ego-driven stuff and on the other is all the meaning. Yes, it was great to be able to build my rugby career up to a certain level – but what's it all mean if you can't also help out the people who make the dream worthwhile?

The old man always said to look after yourself first – because that's the best way to be able to look after others. It's like in a plane when the oxygen masks drop – get yours on first because then you'll be able to help those around you. And then you're in a position where you can also help not just one but many.

I was helping out those closest to me when I played rugby, but since leaving, I've been able to build things in many different areas and help in a lot more ways. That's what it's all about. Just as family is your core, your base. It's who you are. Family is your heart and your strength in this world. Don't forget that.

THE FUTURE

Everyone's looking for that final thing, an outcome, a result or a finish line. But life's not like that. I sure don't see it that way.

Life is constantly evolving, changing. Why would you say, 'I'm not doing that anymore'? A year down the track who knows what's going to appear? It could be a blonde ski bunny lighting a fire in your private lodge in the snow, or better.

So why would you close doors on opportunities in life? You need to keep everything open, and keep the home fires blazing – do that and only good shit will come.

I get bugged about being pigeon-holed. I never look at some tradie and think, 'He's just a plumber'. Is plumbing crap work? Crap work that's got a jet ski in the driveway. That's why if you are a plumber, then I shake my hat in a wide salute given you're now making more coin than a GP. Crap work, hey?

I get it because I get pigeon-holed every day too. I'm 'that Tradies Undies guy'. I'm 'that rugby guy'. I'm The Bachelor. That's part of me, sure, but that's only a very small part of me. Because I am many different things and from here on I'm going to charge into different experiences and scenarios and squeeze every drop out of the future ahead of me.

The first thing I want to do is to put Australia back on the map for the right reasons. Obviously we're on the bloody map, but I want to have more people thinking better about this country and its culture; thinking, 'Yeah, that's a great bloody place', 'Those blokes are wild', and know what it is we're about as a country and a people and a lifestyle.

I want to add to Australia's reputation. The other thing I want to do is to leave this planet a better place than I found it. On a higher level it's about raising the vibrations. It's about putting out some good vibes and changing things up – yeah, that's what I want from the future.

I know a lot of people are struggling right now and will be tomorrow. I want to be that little bit of light, that little bit of a giggle – because a bit of Badger can make a lot of difference, it really can.

THANKS

To accomplish anything worthwhile takes effort and it's a helluva lot easier if like-minded people come along for the ride.

A big thanks to my dad, Mark, for giving me a love for the stories that still make us smile and to my brother Luke for his collection of Aussie slang.

Thanks to Richard Clune for writing down some of these yarns while I was locked up in the Bachelor house.

Thanks to Angus Fontaine for his help and guidance, and to Danielle Walker and Georgia Webb and the team at Pan Macmillan.

Thanks to Nick and the team at The Fordham Company too.

If you get something out of this book, great stuff. If not, use the pages to start the next BBQ.

Take care and see ya round the ridges.

Nick (and Mark)